COUNTRY CHRISTMAS

COUNTRY CHRISTMAS

Exeter Books

NEW YORK

First published in USA 1990
by Exeter Books
Distributed by Bookthrift
Exeter and Bookthrift are registered trademarks of
Siena Publishers Associates New York, New York.

ISBN 0-7917-1605-8

Editors: Francine Lawrence, Jane Newdick
Designer: Georgina Rhodes

NOTES ON THE RECIPES

All recipe measurements give the Metric amount first, followed by the Imperial equivalent. As
these are not exact equivalents, please work from one set of figures. Readers in the United
States should remember that Imperial pints are 20 fluid ounces, whereas U.S. pints are 16 fluid
ounces.
One U.S. cup (8 fluid ounces) is the equivalent of:
100 g/4 oz flour
225 g/8 oz sugar
225 g/8 oz butter

Filmset in Monophoto Garamond by Advanced Filmsetters (Glasgow) Ltd
Printed and bound in Italy by New Interlitho S.p.a., Milan

CONTENTS

FOREWORD

I can remember as a small child the almost unbearable feeling of joy when the same old cardboard box was brought down from the attic and familiar decorations were taken out of their tissue paper. No matter that many were faded or broken, it was important that they were the same as last year and the year before. Then there was the sweet anticipation of opening the advent calendar. Later there were particularly special evenings when, as the eldest of four, I would stay up after my brothers and sister had gone to bed and help my mother to make the mince pies and ice the cake.

We all brought home cards, calendars and presents made at school and Sunday School. Carols were rehearsed for the carol service on squeaky recorders, and Mother's old evening dresses were adapted for the nativity play and pantomime. For the whole of December the kitchen seemed to smell of cinnamon, cloves and baking. Cards arrived and arrangements were made for family visits. It was a long delicious party, and I wanted it to last forever.

Then I began to grow up. As a teenager, I can remember being desperately disappointed in Christmas. All the magic and excitement I had experienced as a young child had gone. It had become predictable. Although Christmas Eve, Christmas Day and Boxing Day were wonderfully different from other days of the year—with neighbours dropping in all day long for a glass of sherry or a potent tot of my father's rum punch and a communal sing-song to guitar and piano accompaniment—there was the tension leading up to the Big Day, which increased each year as everyone's lives grew busier. Worst of all I knew that Santa Claus did not exist.

As I grew older my instincts made me want to run away from Christmas. I compared notes with my friends: something had gone wrong. We in the sophisticated Western world had become caught up in a television soap opera in which Christmas had a price tag on it. We had forgotten what it was really about.

In fact, the enjoyment of Christmas comes as part of the spiritual package. For Christians it is the celebration of the birth of Christ; for others it is the celebration of the family coming together. Busy working people, whether in the town or the country, are tempted to buy many of the decorations, presents and even readymade mince pies. What choice have we when life is so hectic?

In the countryside many people have resisted the commercialism that has overtaken Christmas, and a number of the old traditions still remain. But I wanted to gather together in one book ideas for creating a Christmas that bears more relation to those of our childhood and relies upon simple gestures to show how much family and friends are loved. Cooking is a fundamental way of demonstrating this, and there is a chapter on gloriously Festive Food from Philippa Davenport. Elisabeth Luard has collected favourite Christmas recipes from a family living in the deepest countryside. Jane Newdick has ideas for tree decorations and edible gifts that can be made simply and quickly by all the family. There are also instructions for making more elaborate decorations, as well as a beautiful box to keep them in, which could become heirlooms to pass on to our children.

Christmas is the celebration of Christ's birthday. It is also a just reward for a long and hard year. I do hope that you will enjoy reading and using this book as much as we have enjoyed compiling it.

A very happy and memorable Christmas to you.

Francine Lawrence

CHAPTER 1

THE COUNTRYSIDE IN WINTER

In the dark days of December the countryside can seem uninviting and hostile; bare fields under a lowering sky that threatens to snow may make visitors long for the warmth and company of brightly lit streets crowded with Christmas shoppers. But on a clear winter's day the leafless trees reveal an unsurpassed view, with all the bones of the landscape laid bare. And the hedgerow holly and ivy are a reminder that Christmas is on its way.

When heavy rain turns fields and tracks to mud, or frosts set the earth hard as iron, making the soil unworkable, winter becomes instead a time of maintenance for the farmer. Hedges can be laid or—more usually these days—fences repaired, the barn roof mended and pig sties patched up. After feeding the animals in the morning, the stockman might set out to clear ditches or to fell and saw a tree for a stack of logs for the boiler.

For both man and beast winter has long been a time of living on stored food. Skeins of onions and boxes of apples are stored in the loft above the tractor shed, where the mower and the combine harvester lie idle until the better weather has finally arrived. A few farmers still plant the large, coarse beets known as mangel-wurzels to pull in October and then store in mounds frostproofed with a layer of straw and earth. These 'clamps' are broken open in December and the mangel-wurzels sliced up for appreciative sheep, cows and horses.

On hill farms sheep are brought down to the lowlands for the winter and kept in fields within a short distance of the house. Then when snow falls, the shepherd can still get to his flock to feed them. By Christmas the ewes are heavily in lamb and need extra food to supplement their diet and ensure the development of healthy offspring.

On crisp frosty mornings rabbiting is still a profitable way to pass a few hours, tramping across the fields, armed with a thermos flask of strong tea, a parcel of cheese sandwiches and two ferrets in a wooden box. Purse nets are set across the burrows in the sandy banks under the blackberry bushes and a ferret sent down. Sitting in wait on a still morning you can hear the rabbits moving below the earth, rumbling like an underground train.

A rabbit stuffed with sage and onion graced many a cottage table at Christmas, while on some farms the ritual still persists of killing a pig at Christmas, with the best joints being sent out to sweeten the village policeman or even the bank manager.

Geese were popular for the Christmas table long before turkeys. They are easier to raise and quite capable of fending for themselves: villagers used to graze them on the common and on roadside verges. An old recipe for goose pie recommends that you bone two geese, season them with mace, nutmeg, pepper and salt, and bake them in a raised pie crust with plenty of butter. Anyone who kept a flock of geese would pluck plenty of feathers at Christmas—after they had been roasted in the oven and cleaned, they were ideal for stuffing mattresses and pillows. Quills, made from the flight feathers, and also goose grease were vital materials for the country household.

THE HOLLY BEARS
THE CROWN

Holly has been used for centuries to decorate houses. Silver- or golden-edged leaves of variegated types of holly have a wonderful sparkle and shine in winter, whether they are growing in a garden or used among other evergreens to make Christmas decorations.

Ah the holy growith grene
With ive all alone,
When flowerys can not be sene,
And grene wode levys be gone.

Grene growith the holy,
So doth the ive;
Thow wynter blastys blow never so hye,
Grene growith the holy.

This song is attributed to Henry VIII of England. Written in the 16th century, it expresses the affection felt for this cheerful evergreen. For centuries holly has been gathered to decorate houses. Originally it was to guard them against mischievous spirits—plants that kept their leaves in winter were thought to have magical properties. In Victorian times wreaths hung on the front door were known as welcome rings and consisted of holly, ivy, pine cones and ribbons. The use of ivy, which was associated with femininity, in combination with holly, representing masculinity, promised fertility to the whole household. Today, people still hang wreaths and swags on doors and walls and tuck sprigs of holly above grandfather clocks, picture frames and mirrors.

The Christian church adopted many pagan floral traditions. The red berries of the holly lent themselves to symbolize Christ's blood and suffering, and in Scandinavian countries the holly is known as Christ-thorn. But one plant that the church has always shunned is mistletoe. In Norse legend it was responsible for the death of Balder, the god of light. Druids would cut sprigs of mistletoe with a gold sickle and distribute them as charms against evil. To ward off bad luck, superstitious farmers would feed a piece to a cow that calved at New Year. Some legends cite mistletoe as the tree whose wood was used to build the cross on which Christ was crucified—after which the tree shrunk in shame to become a parasitic shrub. Today's custom of kissing under mistletoe may be connected with the ancient Scandinavians' belief that if enemies met under mistletoe, they would forgive each other and embrace.

Up until the beginning of the 20th century the Christmas rose was cultivated commercially for Christmas trade. The 'rose' is really a hellebore that produces pure white flowers in the depths of winter, and it comes from the mountains of central Europe. When Christmas decorations are taken down after Epiphany, or Twelfth Night, in some

FABLED BEASTS

The reindeer is now fixed in most people's minds as a Christmas animal. Until recently, reindeer ranged across northern Scandinavia and Siberia, but their numbers have been greatly reduced. They are also native to North America, where they are known as caribou; at one time caribou were found in the northern states but are now restricted to Alaska and Canada.

places it is the custom to replace them with Christmas roses and snowdrops, or 'Candlemas bells', to celebrate the Virgin Mary. Rosemary is a plant that is quite forgotten now at Christmas but up until the mid-19th century it played a key part in decorating the house. It was praised for keeping its 'savour all the winter long' and symbolized remembrance and friendship.

At Christmas, houses all over America are decorated with wreaths of greenery; in addition to holly and ivy branches of bay, laurel and evergreen magnolia are used. Bringing pots of poinsettias into the house at Christmas was originally a Mexican custom. If you've ever despaired that your green-fingered skills don't extend to keeping a poinsettia alive, take heart from their Mexican name, *cuextlaxochitl*—it means 'flower that fades'. A Mr Joel Poinsett brought the first plants northwards and from there they were introduced to Europe.

Towards the end of the 19th century a cottage Christmas was a simple affair, just a single day's holiday from work. The farmer would kill an ox and give each of his workers a piece of beef. A good fire would be made, a bottle of home-made wine uncorked and the children given an orange each and a handful of nuts. Some villagers would have taken extra-large joints of meat to the baker's, to be cooked in the ovens still warm from baking the morning's bread.

Up at the 'big' house things were a little different. A band of mummers from the village might call on Christmas Eve and re-enact the battle of St George and the Dragon—a reminder of an age when Christmas was a more rumbustious occasion masterminded by a specially elected Lord of Misrule. The village choir would also call at the 'big' house on Christmas Eve and be rewarded with mince pies and ale for their carol singing.

Before 1650, mince pies were oval in shape, filled with a mixture of shredded meat, suet and dried fruit. They were baked with a pastry baby tucked under the lid, representing Christ in the manger; but under the rule of the Puritans the making of such mince pies was banned as idolatrous. When mince pies returned after the Restoration they were baked in today's familiar round shape.

As well as mince pies, revellers might have been served with Christmas Eve wig cakes. These little buns were flavoured with caraway and peel, and curled over in cooking to resemble an old-fashioned wig. They were

COLD COMFORT

Both man and beast require special adaptations to survive wintry conditions. Reindeer grow long winter coats over a dense, soft underfur, which insulates them from icy Arctic winds. The animals' broad hooves prevent them from floundering in the snow, which is why the idea of reindeer pulling Santa's sleigh is not quite so far-fetched as it may seem. Lapps and Eskimos have always used domesticated reindeer to pull their sleighs. For man, one way of coping with severe weather is found in the steep stone roofs of the row of cottages shown on the right, which shed snow and rain effectively.

traditionally dipped in a hot punch such as lambswool, a mixture of ale and wine drunk through a layer of roast apple, beaten with butter, sugar and nutmeg, that formed the 'lamb's wool'. Possets were also popular at Christmas; they were alcoholic brews mellowed by the addition of eggs and cream—the forerunners of the eggnog traditionally served in the United States at Christmas. Stronger drinks included sloe gin, elderberry port and rum punch.

A fancy iced cake is now served at Christmas but originally the cake was kept until Twelfth Night, when a king and queen were elected by picking cards from a hat. In France—where Twelfth Night is still celebrated—a charm is baked into the cake itself and whoever finds it becomes king or queen for the day. Elsewhere, the feast of Twelfth Night gradually became less and less important and the cake found a place on the Christmas tea table instead.

Santa Claus didn't really come on the scene until the late 19th century, as an amalgamation of European St Nicholas and the English Old Christmas, who was a far less paternal, rather sinister figure. His invention was a reaction to the Puritans' suppression of Christmas in the 1650s, and he was depicted as a wild, drunken, Falstaffian character.

In Austria St Nicholas arrives on December 6th along with the Krampus, his devil-like accomplice. St Nicholas brings presents for good children, and in some villages they leave out a heap of hay for his horse and a glass of brandy to appease the Krampus so that he won't beat them with his stick. Naughty French children can also expect a beating from Père Fouettard, but better-behaved infants leave their shoes in the fireplace for Père Noel (who has now superseded St Nicholas) to fill with gifts. In Dutch households, too, children leave their shoes by the hearth but with a handful of hay or a carrot tucked in for Sinterklaas's horse. Next morning the hay will have vanished and in its place are pink sweets filled with chocolate.

All these European customs crossed the Atlantic with the first settlers, so that Christmas in the United States is a rich blend of traditions. The Dutch settlers first introduced the idea that Santa Claus (the anglicization of Sinterklaas) had a toy workshop at the North Pole.

One of the first mentions of Santa travelling by sleigh pulled by reindeer comes in Clement Clark Moore's poem, 'The Night Before Christmas', published in 1822. Given the location of his workshop, the choice of reindeer was a good one. Lapps and Eskimos have used them for centuries to pull sleighs and as pack animals—the animals' large spreading hooves mean that they can travel safely across deep snow whereas horses or donkeys would flounder.

CHRISTMAS IS COMING
THE GOOSE IS GETTING FAT

The goose had a fine and long tradition as a bird for festive tables until the turkey usurped its position. The goose was both a humble and a royal bird, gracing the table of peasant and king alike. Apart from the rich and delicious flesh it provided for celebration feasts, other parts, such as quills, feathers and grease, were vital for the running of the country household.

Christmas crackers arrived in England via France. In 1847 Tom Smith, an apprentice confectioner, copied the sugared almonds wrapped in twists of tissue paper he had seen in Paris. They didn't really catch on until he had the idea of adding a bang by wrapping up the sweets with a friction strip.

The Christmas tree too originated in Europe, this time Germany. German settlers took the tradition to the United States in the 17th century. Children in Pennsylvania, one of the main German settlements, decorated trees with cranberries, apples, animal-shaped cookies and garlands made from popcorn strung on thread. From then on, the Christmas tree became increasingly popular in the United States. Today an old-fashioned, 'country-style' tree is more likely to be decorated with candy canes and flags than cranberries or apples, but Christmas cookies are still made in many different shapes—some to eat and some purely for decoration. Strings of popcorn are still sometimes used, and decorations made from calico.

In Britain Christmas trees didn't really become popular until the 1840s, when Prince Albert's fondness for spectacularly decorated trees inspired the nation. Victorian Christmas trees were decorated with candles, cakes, sweets and paper chains. Electric fairylights were introduced in the 1890s. By this time, the Christmas tree had caught on in several other European countries as well.

The fashion in Britain was helped along by the publication of Charles Dickens's *A Christmas Carol*, which set down all the traditions of a family fireside Christmas. Some of the customs he described were relatively unknown, but middle-class families on both sides of the Atlantic were quick to adopt them.

Round about the same time, antiquarians travelled the country collecting and writing down carols dating from medieval times. The Victorians wrote plenty of carols of their own but with a religious theme missing from the older songs.

The Christmas card also appeared in Victorian times. The first one was designed in England in 1843 and may have been inspired by the custom of embellishing visiting cards with seasonal designs at Christmas and New Year. However, the idea did not really catch on until 1870—when the Post Office introduced a half-price tariff for unsealed cards. The first American cards were designed in Boston at about this time.

A traditional Christmas as we picture it today only really evolved in Victorian times, and was an exercise in nostalgia even then. The tradition of gift-giving, however, goes back to the gifts of the Magi to the infant Jesus on the day of Epiphany. The giving of gifts, along with feasting and good fellowship has always been at the heart of the festive season, and nowhere more than in the countryside.

SHEPHERDS ABIDING IN THE FIELDS

Animals have always been part of the Christmas story. They feature in many carols and songs, and our idea of a stable in Bethlehem is not complete without an ox and ass and sheep and lambs. The image of Mary riding a donkey wearily towards Bethlehem is strong and enduring, as is the picture of the shepherds wondering at the miracle that has occurred. The shepherd's job has changed significantly since sheep were watched on Bethlehem hills, but the work involved in caring for a flock retains many of the invaluable old skills from earlier centuries.

CHAPTER 2

DECK THE HALLS WITH BOUGHS OF HOLLY

HOLLY AND IVY AND MISTLETOE, GIVE ME A RED APPLE AND LET ME GO

Woods, hedgerows and gardens offer tremendous scope for Christmas decorations. There are branches of soft fir and sombre yew, gleaming holly and graceful ivy, red-berried leafless branches and mysterious yellow-green mistletoe, perhaps a few special sprigs of herbs and scented flowers, and a spray or two of winter jasmine or hellebore to add colour to a background of deep green.

This abundance of material can be cut and woven into all manner of decorations, from a sophisticated garland twining down a staircase, to a simpler kissing bunch of mistletoe hung near a doorway; from a spectacular wreath made from a variety of fresh evergreen leaves, to an informal swag.

Fruits and nuts and berries become the jewels to set among the branches. Pine cones and dried seed heads can be used either in their natural state or lightly brushed with gold or silver to add a discreet touch of sparkle. During the months leading up to Christmas, collect things you find on walks and in the garden and set them somewhere safe to dry so that you will have a store to make decorations from. The range of flowers, foliage, and seedheads that can be preserved in various ways is astonishing.

Branches of fir, ivy, holly and other evergreens are best picked about a day before you need to use them. Strip away their lower leaves and crush or split woody stems, then stand the branches in a bucket of water for at least 12 hours to give them a good drink. In the winter months these tough, mature leaves will last well out of water, but they still relish a long drink before being arranged. Remember to keep one perfect sprig of berried holly aside to decorate the Christmas pudding in the traditional way.

NATURAL ALTERNATIVES

A vast assortment of leaves, fruits and berries, such as those shown on the right, can be collected from garden and hedgerow to make swags, garlands and bunches. Tartan, which has become a Christmas classic, looks superb with acid green limes, holly and yew twining down a staircase, as shown on the previous two pages.

GREAT RICHES

Fresh winter fruits, fragrant dried herbs and spices, simple cream candles and soft green moss from the forest floor can be combined with evergreen leaves and berries to make rich and wonderful decorations. Stand a simple pyramid of fruit among leaves and berries, or make a nest of creamy candles—which can be either plain or scented—in a basket of moss. None of these ideas is difficult to do, and the result will look superb either as a table centrepiece or standing on a side table or low chest through the days of Christmas.

S P I C E   T R E E

S I M P L E   S W E D I S H   C A N D L E S

In a warm room this little tree gives out a delicious spicy scent. Use a pyramid-shaped base of floral foam soaked until wet. Stand this in a terracotta plant pot saucer and cover the foam with short sprigs of yew and variegated holly. Wire together clusters of cinnamon sticks, vanilla pods, whole nutmegs, dried mushrooms or curls of dried citrus peel, and push these in among the foliage. Finish off with wired bows of tartan ribbon. Stand the arrangement on a small circular table and surround it with rosy polished apples and an edging of yew fronds.

Line a shallow, rustic basket with aluminium foil or cling film (plastic wrap) to make a waterproof container. Fill the basket with a thick layer of bun moss (a type of moss that grows in clumps on banks and stone roofs, or can be ordered from florists). For the most natural effect, do not remove small twigs and leaves that are attached to the velvety moss. Tuck in among the moss a collection of short, fat, creamy-coloured candles. Stand the basket in a corner of a room but keep it safely away from curtains when you light the candles.

TANGERINE PYRAMID

A china or glass compotier can be decorated lavishly for Christmas. Pile it with layers of shiny winter tangerines or oranges. If the fruits don't have their own foliage attached, then tuck in spikes of fresh bay leaves or any small glossy evergreen leaves to the top of each fruit. Add clusters of velvety cob nuts (filberts) in their skins, and sprinkle with brilliant orangey-red rosehips to add sparkle. This sumptuous mixture would make a wonderful dessert for a Christmas meal or it could simply stand on a side table as a rich, glowing decoration for the twelve nights of Christmas.

BURNISHED FRUITS

The rough-textured, inedible skin of pinkish-brown lychees looks wonderful sponged with a hint of gold, as shown overleaf. The little fruits can then be used as an edible decoration—either spread out in gold-edged paper cases, or wired and hung on wreaths or on the Christmas tree. The shiny paper leaves (gold cake decorations) add the finishing touch.

GILDED WREATH

Use a ready-made vine wreath as the base for this, attaching gilded leaves, whole nuts, poppy seed heads and little clusters of dried rosehips to it. Collect and press flat dead leaves such as maple and sycamore, and search for the naturally dry and stiff leaves that drop from magnolia or laurel. Sponge a very light covering of gold over the leaves so that they still look natural. Touch the tops of poppy seed heads and the shells of whole walnuts or pecans with gold. A glue gun is the best method for attaching these things, but they could be wired in place instead if you do not have access to a glue gun or have not used one before. The finishing touch is added with tiny gilded marzipan pears which are wired with thin rose wire in among the leaves so that the wire is hidden. The stiffened golden fabric bow adds a touch of frivolity to the sculptural simplicity of the wreath.

FANTASTICAL TREE

A lichen-covered leafless branch of elder, some floral foam and a well-worn terracotta flower pot are the basis for this magical tree. Push the branch securely into the foam inside the pot, taping it in place if necessary. Hang gold-painted plastic birds and gold paper leaves from the bare branches with fine rose wire. Make marzipan pears from white marzipan moulded into pear shapes, with a clove at each end to look like a stalk and calyx. Hang these too from the branches with fine rose wire. Stand the tree where it can catch some sparkle from candlelight for a truly fantastical effect.

A TOUCH OF GOLD

*D*ry *winter twigs and crisp brown leaves can be turned into magical decorations with the lightest touch of a gilding brush or sponge. A discreet sparkle complements perfectly the rich and natural colours of material from fields and gardens. Bronze powders bought loose in a variety of shades, or ready mixed into a paint medium, provide the most subtle and delicious range of golds. These can be gently brushed or sponged on to fresh or dried leaves, nuts, twigs, seed heads, berries, pine cones and spices. Here, autumn leaves, painted gold, form the basis of a table centre of fruits, nuts, dried rosehips and a gilded poppy seedhead.*

RICH FABRICS

*U*sing quite small pieces and off-cuts of sumptuous fabrics together can create rich and lavish effects. Here strongly contrasting colours in silk taffetas and dupions are layered over small round tables as a background for piles of glowing fruits and decorations. Lengths of gold star chains sold as tree decorations loop around a candlestick to make a glittering centrepiece and add to the Renaissance look.

CLASSIC CHRISTMAS WREATH

The shape of a traditional wreath suggests continuity and wholeness. The comforting circular outline hanging on a door or wall offers the prospect of a warm and friendly welcome, and a homemade one, however simple, is much more personal than any ready-made wreath. To make a wreath which will last for ten days or so and still look fresh, you must use a base that will stay moist. This serves as a reservoir from which the leaves can take up water. The classic way to do this is to wire damp moss on to a frame, as explained below. A very much quicker method is to soak a bought floral-foam ring until damp, and then simply push short sprigs of evergreens into the foam. You can use a combination of fresh and dried materials in a wreath, but if it is to hang outside, choose the less delicate dried materials, such as dried poppy heads or glycerined eucalyptus. A sheltered porch is a perfect position for a wreath made from a mixture of more fragile dried flowers or leaves and fresh material, since it is protected yet is still cool enough to keep the evergreens looking fresh.

As well as the traditional red and green wreath, think about other colour combinations. For instance, blue fir looks stunning with dried hydrangea flowers and blue bows. Clusters of rosebuds that have been preserved in silica gel are exquisite against a background of moss.

1 2 3

MATERIALS
wire wreath base

loose sphagnum moss

roll of mossing wire

sprigs of evergreen leaves

stub wires

small pieces of dried hydrangea heads (see Note)

rosehips or other suitable berries

NOTE: Hydrangea flowerheads can be dried in early autumn when already partially dry and papery. Cut them with a good stem, and stand in 5 cm (2 inches) of water in a vase for a week to ten days. The water prevents the flowerhead from wilting as it dries.

TO MAKE
1 Soak the loose moss for a few hours in water. Squeeze out the excess moisture and cover the wire base thickly with the moss, wiring it in place as you work and building up a good, solid covering.

2 Snip off short lengths of ivy, holly or whatever foliage you are using from larger branches. Push them into the moss, tucking ends of stems under wire where possible. Aim to cover the whole ring evenly, covering the inner and outer edges completely.

3 Attach short lengths of stub wire to little clusters of berries and to small pieces of dried hydrangea florets using the fine mossing wire. Push the wired berries and flowers into the moss among the foliage, spreading them evenly throughout the wreath. Add as many decorative bits and pieces as you like, but keep the whole effect as natural and subtle as possible for a country look. Attach a loop of wire through the back of the base to hang the wreath from a door. The completed wreath should last for a week or more outside in a sheltered position such as in a front porch.

WREATH ON FRONT COVER: To make the wreath shown on the front cover, combine deep-green holly, ivy, viburnum and choisya leaves on a wire base covered with damp moss. Add sharp notes of colour with berries and fruits such as clusters of fresh or dried rosehips, crab apples and ivy flowers. Finish with discreet tartan ribbon bows.

A TRUCE BY THE TREE OF CANDLELIGHT

Bringing a living fir tree indoors to decorate for Christmas is quite a new tradition, as traditions go. In both England and North America it did not really become popular until Victorian times. The first decorations were probably homemade, but elaborate and beautiful glass ornaments quickly became available, and strings of beads and glittering metal tinsel turned the plain green fir into a fairytale tree.

Candles (although still used widely in Scandinavia) have mostly given way to electric lights now, which are of course a great deal safer, and the choice of tree decorations is vast. Yet the decorations you make yourself have a charm and meaning beyond sophisticated glitter. Gingerbread biscuit shapes and folded paper cut-outs, strings of berries and gilded nuts, tangerines and polished apples, embroidered decorations and

sprays of dried flowers look marvellous. (A recipe for gingerbread biscuit shapes, and instructions for embroidered decorations are given on pages 48 and 70 respectively.) They can be used on their own, or mixed with well-loved and treasured decorations collected down the years. The choice of a fairy or a star atop the tree is usually left to the children in the family, and decorating the tree is one job at Christmas that they love to take over.

Children enjoy being involved in the busy preparation time before Christmas. As well as making decorations for the tree, they can print wrapping papers, cards and tags and cook simple biscuits and sweets to give as presents. Competitions to see who can make the longest paper chain in the shortest time are also very popular.

VICTORIAN THEME

A rich, sumptuous Victorian look is well suited to a traditional country Christmas. The splendid arrangement on the previous two pages consists of gilded and exotic fruit, flowers, leaves and seedheads, accented by gilded cinnamon sticks. The spectacular tree on the right is decorated with Victorian card cut-outs, fat red apples, plain white candle lights, bunches of spices and nuts. The fir-covered mantelpiece above provides a base for red apples, frosty sprays of dried sea lavender, pine cones, fat white pleated paper bows, and clusters of tiny golden glass grapes.

CHAPTER 3

WE WISH YOU A MERRY CHRISTMAS

Homemade presents are the gifts which get remembered, whether they are a child's first clumsy attempt at sewing or cooking or a more sophisticated something dreamed up by a friend to reach your weak spot. They can be quite simple or rich and luxurious, but what will shine through are the thought and love and care that have gone into them. Carry through the homemade theme with wrapping paper and labels decorated by printing or spongeing. Both are old-fashioned and effective ways of making something beautiful from the plainest materials.

Gifts of food are always welcome, especially if they are the kind of things which take time and trouble to make normally or are simple to make but expensive to buy. Someone living alone or a small household of two would welcome a small but rich and delicious Christmas cake, chocolate truffles or spiced nuts, while a large household with lots of ravenous children would be thrilled with a huge box of home-baked biscuits.

Presents like jellies, sophisticated fruit liqueurs or herb vinegars need to have been planned and made earlier in the year when the garden offers an abundance of fruit and vegetables, but there are still plenty of things which can be produced within a week or two of being given away. Subtly spiced chutneys are delicious made from dried fruits, and seasonal kumquats can be immersed in a potent syrup laced with brandy or orange liqueur.

Other gift ideas for a gourmet include grainy mustard spiked with fresh chillies, or traditional sauces such as Cumberland sauce to eat with cold baked ham. The best results in every case will come from using the best raw ingredients. However simple the recipe, always use the finest materials and you will have presents which you are proud to give away and which are a delight to receive.

Above: Children love to get involved with present making and wrapping and labelling the finished gifts.
Right: The days before Christmas spent in the kitchen cooking delicious gifts are some of the best of the season.

GILDED OFFERINGS

The past offers a rich source of inspiration for homemade gifts. In medieval times small, spiced biscuits were baked and decorated for special occasions. Cloves and tiny leaves were studded into the surface and gilded to represent heraldic symbols. This idea can be copied in a more up-to-date way using edible gold paints or gold foil. Cut shapes using metal cutters; or for special biscuits such as these angels, make a cardboard template and cut out the dough using a small, pointed knife. Pure gold leaf or a less expensive substitute can be laid on to the cool, cooked biscuits, using egg white as a glue. Alternatively, simply use cloves, currants or gold and silver balls for decoration.

It is possible to buy gold food colouring but this is not as rich and shiny as other gold paints. The gingerbread recipe to make these shapes can be adapted to adult or children's tastes by adding or taking away ginger and spices to just the right degree. If you intend to bake a batch of biscuits to give away, experiment a little first until you get the flavour you think the recipient will enjoy. Children would probably prefer biscuits piped with white icing or initials or names written on the surface rather than the more sophisticated gold decoration. If all this decoration is too fiddly, then simply leave the shapes plain and glossy—they will still taste delicious.

Store or pack gingerbread biscuits in an airtight container to keep them crisp. They can go soft in a moist atmosphere but are just as good when chewy rather than brittle.

The presentation of edible gifts is almost as important as their taste. Old glass jars and bottles can be embellished with gold glass-paint or foil. You can pick out a raised design on the surface or simply paint a trail of stylized leaves or flowers around a plain bottle. Make sure that everything is labelled well with storage instructions if they are relevant. Dip the edges of paper *petit four* cases into gold paint for a sparkling finish, and pack sweets into pretty boxes among shredded tissue paper or gold lametta. Make use of gold paper doilies and cake decorations to decorate packaging for candies and cakes to give a really luxurious finishing touch.

Miniature ready-made paper carrier bags make instant wrappings for last-minute edible gifts, the sort you take somewhere and give straightaway. If the contents are not to be eaten then and there, pack them first in a sealed cellophane twist or bag before slipping it into the outer bag. If chocolates or rich biscuits (cookies) are packed into boxes to be kept for a while, make sure that all the materials you use as packaging are harmless and won't taint the food in any way. Find special waxed papers and make use of cellophane or foils to prevent oils from seeping out into the paper or cardboard and spoiling the look of the gift. All kinds of containers can be pressed into use for displaying edible presents. Small, shallow baskets are particularly good; well lined and finished off with cellophane, they remain useful long after the contents have been eaten.

Above: Spicy gingerbread shapes come packed in shiny gold paper bags.
Make extra amounts and hang on the Christmas tree to give to visitors.
Right: Invent your own special shapes and designs such as these
triumphant angels floating beside stars and moons on
a deep wooden plate.

MINIATURE CHRISTMAS CAKES

This recipe makes a golden rather than a dark cake. When cool, the cakes can be iced with conventional icing. Or they can be brushed with honey, decorated with whole nuts, glacé cherries, crystallized ginger and fruits, then glazed again with honey. Makes six 10 cm (4 inch) tins or two 20 cm (8 inch) tins.

350 g/12 oz yellow sultanas (golden raisins)
100 g/4 oz raisins
225 g/8 oz crystallized pineapple, coarsely chopped
100 g/4 oz crystallized ginger, coarsely chopped
100 g/4 oz angelica, coarsely chopped
350 g/12 oz whole candied peel, finely chopped
450 g/1 lb glacé (candied) cherries, coarsely chopped
75 ml/6 tbsp sherry or brandy
450 g/1 lb butter
450 g/1 lb caster (superfine) sugar
grated rind of 1 orange
grated rind and juice of 2 lemons
8 eggs, beaten till very foamy
450 g/1 lb plain (all-purpose) flour
100 g/4 oz walnuts, coarsely chopped
100 g/4 oz almonds, coarsely chopped

Thoroughly grease six 10 cm (4 inch) tins, or two 20 cm (8 inch) tins, then line them with a double thickness of greaseproof paper (waxed paper). Tie several thicknesses of brown paper around the outside of the tins, coming up higher than the tops; line them too.
Soak the chopped fruit in the sherry or brandy for a few hours.
Cream the butter, sugar and orange and lemon rind until very fluffy. Add the beaten egg a little at a time. Add a spoonful of the flour if the mixture begins to curdle. Fold in the flour then the lemon juice. Carefully add the fruits and nuts and any soaking liquid remaining. Put mixture into prepared tins, making a hollow in the centre of the mixture.
Bake in the oven at 180°C/350°F/mark 4 for about 45 minutes, then lower the temperature to 140°C/275°F/mark 1 and bake for a further 1½ hours. Watch the cakes carefully, taking them out of the oven when evenly risen and brown, and the edges have shrunk slightly from edge of tin. The time taken will depend on your oven and on the depth of the cake mixture. For two 20 cm (8 inch) tins, lengthen the cooking time to about 4–4½ hours in total. Cool in the tins for an hour or more.

GINGERBREAD SHAPES

By varying the proportions of black treacle (molasses) and golden syrup, you can make biscuits in many shades of brown. The recipe makes enough biscuits to decorate a whole Christmas tree.

175 g/6 oz soft brown sugar
60 ml/4 tbsp golden syrup (corn syrup)
30 ml/2 tbsp black treacle (molasses)
grated rind of ½ orange
grated rind of ½ lemon
200 g/7 oz butter, diced
5 ml/1 tsp bicarbonate of soda (baking soda)
450 g/1 lb plain (all-purpose) flour
10 ml/2 tsp ground cinnamon
5 ml/1 tsp ground nutmeg
10 ml/2 tsp ground ginger
2.5 ml/½ tsp ground allspice

Grease some large baking sheets. In a large saucepan bring the sugar, golden syrup, treacle (molasses), 30 ml/2 tbsp water and orange and lemon rinds to the boil, stirring well. Remove pan from heat and add the butter and the bicarbonate of soda (baking soda). Stir in the flour and spices gradually until you have a smooth dough. If it seems very wet, add a little more flour; it will stiffen as it cools. Leave for about an hour.
On a large floured board roll out the dough to a thickness of about 3 mm/⅛ inch. Cut out the shapes using a cardboard template or sharp metal cutters. Put the shapes on baking trays, leaving enough space for them to spread.
Bake in the oven at 180°C/350°F/mark 4 for 10–12 minutes until firm but not too dark. Leave to cool for 5 minutes before removing to wire racks.
If you want to hang the gingerbread shapes on the Christmas tree, cut a hole in each just before or just after baking.

FRUIT, NUT AND SEED CHOCOLATES

These take only about 10 minutes to make and are absolutely delicious.

50 g/2 oz almonds, finely chopped
25 g/1 oz pine kernels, finely chopped
50 g/2 oz sesame seeds
100 g/4 oz pumpkin seeds, finely chopped
100 g/2 oz raisins, finely chopped
5 ml/1 tsp ground cinnamon
2.5 ml/½ tsp ground cloves
peel of 1 large orange
225 g/8 oz white chocolate

Stir-fry the nuts and seeds in a frying pan without oil until toasted. When cool, put in a bowl with raisins, spices and orange peel. Melt the white chocolate and pour into dry ingredients. Stir well and spoon heaps of the mixture into paper cases. Leave to set.

Right: Rich Chocolate Truffles line up in a frivolous gift box edged with gold paper.

SPICED PEARS

These make an attractive present when packed into a large glass storage jar and are delicious with Christmas meats and poultry.

1.8 kg/4 lb firm pears, peeled
cloves
550 g/1½ lb demerara (light brown) sugar
1.1 litres/2 pints white wine vinegar
pared rind of a lemon
small piece of root ginger
2 cinnamon sticks
10 ml/2 tsp whole mace

Stud each pear with 2 or 3 cloves. Put in a large pan. Dissolve the sugar in the vinegar, and pour over the pears. Add rind and spices, and bring to the boil. Simmer until pears look transparent.

Remove pears and drain before putting into clean, hot jars.

Simmer vinegar mixture until reduced and thick and syrupy. Pour over pears and seal lids. Store for a few weeks to allow the flavours to mellow.

APRICOT LIQUEUR

good-quality dried apricots
vodka or brandy
1 or 2 cinnamon sticks
almonds
cane sugar

Soak apricots in a small amount of water to plump them up. Pack into jars and pour vodka or brandy over them. Add cinnamon stick, a few almonds and a little sugar. Leave for several weeks, either turning or shaking the jar occasionally.

Strain off the liquid to drink as a liqueur, and eat the apricots as a dessert.

KUMQUATS WITH GRAND MARNIER

kumquats
sugar
orange-flavoured liqueur, such as Grand Marnier

Blanch kumquats in a small amount of boiling water for about a minute, then simmer for ten minutes. Drain the fruit and pack into hot, clean jars. Pour over them a syrup made from 350 g/12 oz sugar to 300 ml/½ pint water. To each jar add at least 30 ml/2 tbsp (or a miniature bottle) of the liqueur. Seal and keep for up to 1 week.

MARZIPAN STUFFED DATES

fresh dates, stoned (pitted)
homemade marzipan
demerara (light brown) sugar

Fill centre of each date with a wedge of homemade marzipan. Roll in demerara (light brown) sugar.

Put in petit four cases.

CHOCOLATE-COVERED MARZIPAN LOGS

100 g/4 oz good-quality candied orange peel, finely chopped
15 ml/1 tbsp orange-flavoured liqueur, such as Grand Marnier
250 g/9 oz homemade marzipan
plain chocolate
white vegetable fat
pistachio nuts

Knead the finely chopped orange peel, along with the orange-flavoured liqueur, into the marzipan.

Break off small pieces and roll into log shapes. Allow to harden slightly.

Melt the chocolate in a double boiler; a tiny piece of white vegetable fat melted with the chocolate keeps it flowing freely and sets with a gloss.

Dip the log shapes in the melted chocolate. Decorate each with a pistachio nut and leave to set on non-stick paper.

RICH CHOCOLATE TRUFFLES

The better the chocolate you use the more delicious the truffles will be. Too sweet a chocolate will produce over sickly results.

500 g/1 lb plain chocolate, chopped into small pieces
200 ml/7 fl oz single cream
25 g/1 oz unsalted butter
45 ml/3 tbsp Cognac, Kirsch or other liqueur
cocoa powder, for dusting

Put the cream and butter into a heavy-based saucepan and bring to the boil. Take the pan off the heat and add the chopped chocolate. Stir thoroughly until all the chocolate has melted. Add the liqueur spoonful by spoonful, stirring well.

Pour the mixture into a shallow tray lined with non-stick paper. Leave in a cool place for several hours. Cut into small squares with a sharp knife.

Leave some squares as they are and dip some into cocoa powder.

It is best to store these truffles in the refrigerator if they are to be kept for any length of time. Pack them into boxes in single layers, alternating rows of plain truffles and cocoa-dusted truffles.

Left: *Attention to detail and clever packaging can turn quite simple edible gifts into luxurious presents. Even the most strong-willed are likely to succumb to the pleasures of chocolate, fruit and liqueurs at Christmas.*
Overleaf: *Basic brown paper and dry autumn leaves get the gold treatment with sponge and brush.*

ALL WRAPPED UP

First impressions count, and a present wrapped lovingly and with special care adds immeasurably to the pleasure and anticipation felt by the recipient. Wrappings do not have to be lavish or glossy, but attention to small details and an overall pretty effect makes opening a gift a treat in itself.

Straightforward materials such as brown parcel wrapping paper and old-fashioned string can be transformed with a brush of paint or a simple block print and a blob or two of real sealing wax. If children want to help, arrange for them to do some simple printing or spongeing on rolls of inexpensive cream lining paper or parcel paper. In one short session they will decorate enough paper to wrap all the presents you have waiting.

Choose a simple idea for the maximum effect, such as stencilling through a paper doilie or cutting a single star or tree shape in a potato or piece of pumpkin and using this as a block printer. You can buy small wooden blocks with slightly more complicated designs to do border patterns or neater rows of motifs.

Look out for unbleached and recycled paper to work on if you are using it in quantity. For a few special presents buy a basic coloured paper for gold stencilling and printing. There are dozens of different types of gold paint available, ranging from water-based poster paints and inks to powerful lacquers and sprays. Some of the best effects are obtained by using loose bronze powders mixed into a paint medium and then brushed or sponged on to a surface. Alternatively, the loose powder can be sprinkled or shaken on to a fixing medium or glue. The bronze powders come in a range of colours from reddish coppers to yellow golds. All gold paints are made from metal powders suspended in a base, but some are actually much shinier and richer-looking than others. A small phial or packet of powder will go a long way, especially as it looks best used quite sparingly. Mix only small amounts of powders into the medium in shallow saucers or jar lids.

One of the most dramatic paper effects is achieved by spongeing one or more gold paints on to brown paper. A small piece of natural sponge is best for doing this. Just dip it into the paint and then press it on to the paper at random.

You can create elegant stripes simply by dragging a paintbrush dipped in one colour, such as gold, in one direction, then dragging a second paintbrush dipped in another colour, such as copper, in the opposite direction, between the first stripes.

Or use paintbrushes to drizzle paint on to the paper to produce a spattered effect. For a particularly subtle finish, dip a stencil brush in the paint, dab the brush on absorbent kitchen paper to remove most of it, then flick the brush with your thumb to make tiny specks.

If you are skilled and artistic you might like to try cutting a lino or scraper board design to print your own papers and labels. A quicker, easier and less nerve-wracking way to a similar result is to buy wooden blocks—or simply use a potato.

Usually considered to be the kind of thing children get up to at nursery school, potato printing is fun and effective. It may not be sophisticated but anyone can do it. Pumpkins, which some consider superior to the humble potato, provide a larger surface area. Don't try too complicated a pattern; if it is something very simple, such as a star, aim for a slightly wild and uncontrolled image. If you start to make a motif symmetrical and perfectly measured, the whole process becomes too fiddly and the spontaneity is lost.

Cut the potato in half, mark the motif and cut around it, so that the motif is about 6 mm ($\frac{1}{4}$ inch) higher than the rest. Use an enamel or china plate to mix the paint to the correct consistency. Thick paint works best with potatoes, but use only a small amount—blot off the excess before printing.

Wooden blocks work with most paints, but sometimes proper printing inks give a neater result. Experiment and find the materials which suit you. Work quickly to produce a kind of rhythm—often a random pattern is far easier to achieve than a very ordered one.

Right: You can recycle old glass jars, bottles and containers to hold
gifts using gold foils and paints. Here, presents are wrapped in
gold-sponged paper and trimmed with gold foil, and a port bottle is
embellished with a trail of leaves and a hand-written label.

CHAPTER 4

CHRISTMAS KEEPSAKES

One of the greatest delights of Christmas, especially for children, is to bring down from the attic or from the back of a cupboard the box containing decorations and special things kept for Christmas each year. The things that were carefully packed away last year come out looking magically different. Fresh and unexpected, they seem to hold in them all the excitement and anticipation that will infect the household right up to the day itself.

They are like old friends that one is pleased to see. Many families add a few new things each year to the colourful, glittery treasure: perhaps a new tree decoration, a special cushion or candlestick, armfuls of tinsel and paper chains, or another figure for the nativity scene. Over the years a wonderful store of family memories is built up, with each person having his or her favourite decoration.

Beautiful, hand-made items make the box even more special, and in this chapter there are instructions for charming Christmas decorations to make in the weeks before Christmas. A pleasure to make and a delight to use, they can be brought out with the Christmas box every year and could even become treasured family heirlooms.

With such a revival of interest in the old-fashioned decorative skills of stencilling, this chapter includes special Christmas stencils by Lyn Le Grice. They are shown here used on fabric and paper but could also be stencilled on to a screen or piece of furniture.

There is also a revival of interest these days in gilding and painting techniques, which can be put to good use with the magical painted box featured in this chapter. Use it to store all the special Christmas things you want to keep safe and together—which is much better than pushing everything into worn-out cardboard cartons that get squashed at the back of a cupboard.

The hanging tree decorations are perfect for anyone who loves doing tapestry or embroidery. But if that seems too difficult or fiddly, the idea of simple stuffed fabric shapes to hang on the tree could easily be adapted. You could make the shapes completely from felt, scraps of silk or satin, or any rich or attractive material, and then sew on to the surface tiny beads, miniature ribbon bows or any other decoration that inspires you. Bind the edges, or add gold cord exactly as for the tapestry shapes shown on page 70. If you like to stick to a stylish one- or two-colour scheme for your Christmas tree, then you could make the decorations in colours to suit it.

Similarly, you could adapt the Christmas cushion featured in this chapter if you do not have the sewing skills or the time to make this version. Simply using tartan fabrics or some of the many pretty cotton Christmas prints available, make several cushion covers to slip over existing cushions. Patchwork covers from seasonal fabrics would look good, or you could just make plain and simple covers. If you do not like putting in zips, then use fabric ties or a row of buttons instead to make the closure.

While you are sewing, it would be a good chance to make some special napkins and perhaps a tablecloth for everyday meals using Christmassy fabrics or a bold and festive colour scheme. Small details such as these are what make every Christmas individual and special to one household, and they are the kind of thing children remember and treasure for years to come.

Children can help make things too, especially in the days leading up to Christmas when they are excited and need to be occupied. A Christmas crib is something that they can put together easily from bits and pieces around the house; the people and animals can be modelled or cast and painted or dressed in scraps.

The professionalism and finish are not what counts with any of these things made to be kept. Rather, it is the feeling that whoever spent careful hours creating something, has actually enjoyed the making, has felt that it was time well spent and in so doing has given pleasure to everyone else who has seen or used it. Country people at one time would naturally have made things to decorate their homes despite spending long days working. Although this was obviously partly out of necessity, they did know the satisfaction and pleasure to be gained from it. We too would do well to find time for something so rewarding.

Right: Crisp Irish linen has been decorated with a stencilled Christmas motif to make a fabulous table setting for the most important meal of the year.
Overleaf: The subtle corals, blue-greens and dull gold used for the stencil design echo the warm Christmas colours from rich fruits, dried flowers and spicy biscuits which decorate the dining room.

SEASONAL STENCILS

Stencilling is one of the best ways of decorating all kinds of surfaces and materials quickly and stylishly. It is a craft that can reward with dramatic results even if you are a complete beginner. Practice makes perfect, but first attempts can be exciting too. It is an excellent way to create Christmas decorations, and once you have cut a stencil and are armed with plenty of paints, you can make a stack of wrapping paper in an afternoon, or transform a plain white linen tablecloth.

Lyn Le Grice's Christmas stencil is based on a twiggy garland entwined with mistletoe, ivy, evergreens and trailing ribbons. The colours are soft and unusual—a subtle almond green, brick and coral with highlights of gold used with restraint. Lyn always uses spray paints, building up colour slowly with quick bursts of spray that leave just a hint of paint. She mixes pale washes in all the colours she is using to create a subtle, merging, shadowy effect. This style of stencilling is a far cry from solid colour stippled heavily through simple, repetitive cut-outs and is easier to execute from pre-cut stencils. If you wish to cut your own, try a

simpler design like the holly motif overleaf. Once the knack of spraying lightly and gently has been understood the creative possibilities are limitless.

Spraying paints through stencils means that you can decorate many different types of surfaces, including cotton fabrics, wood, ceramic, and walls, so long as they are flat enough to position and hold the stencil against while you fill in the colour.

A large, pure white, Irish linen tablecloth made the perfect background for Lyn's Christmas stencil. Large square matching napkins, each with the garland stencilled on to them, can be used either conventionally as dinner napkins or as place mats on top of the tablecloth. It doesn't matter if each stencilling isn't quite the same as the last one, as a slightly haphazard look somehow adds to the richness of the overall effect. Lyn stencilled two motifs in the centre of the large cloth, but they could be arranged differently to suit the size and shape of your own table or even stencilled around the edge of the tablecloth.

Above: Soft tissue papers can be
subtly stencilled with a Christmas
design. Use them for wrapping
delicate presents and lining gift boxes
or baskets.

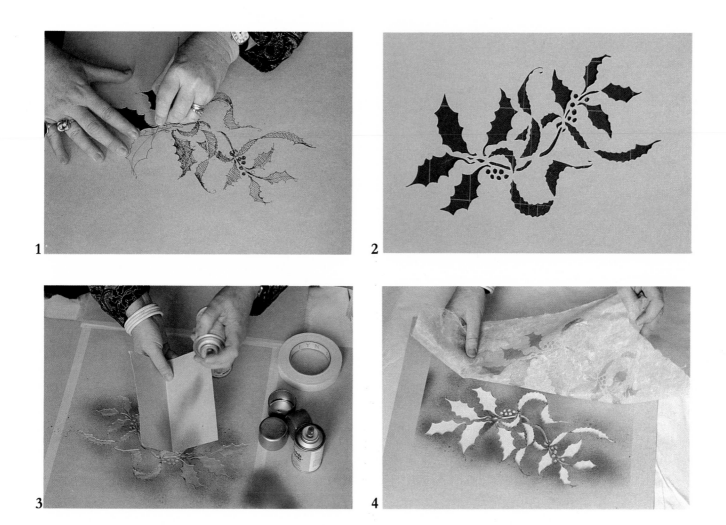

PREPARING A STENCIL

1 Decide on your design and draw it on the stencil cardboard. Using a scalpel or stencil knife, cut as smoothly as possible. To turn a corner, move the stencil not the blade.

2 Always cut and work on a proper work mat to prevent the cardboard from slipping. After cutting stencil, spray a fine film of mounting adhesive on to back of stencil.

3 Put stencil in place and begin spraying colour in short, light bursts, building up colour strength gradually. Block out areas with cardboard to control where paint goes.

4 Carefully remove stencil from material, or if fabric or paper is flimsy, pull it gently from the stencil cardboard. Clean stencil and store for further use.

FESTIVE FIRESIDES

At Christmas more than at any other time of the year, an open fire becomes the focus of attention. It is the place to sit and open presents together, drink a toast or roast chestnuts in the embers. It can be a place of quiet escape to read a book or simply sit and watch the flames and remember Christmases past.

Most people decorate their houses with temporary decorations, but these days few think to make something which is more lasting, as these are. In the past, and especially in rural communities, people cut and sewed scraps to make Christmas banners and pictures to hang above a fireplace or on a wall, often embellished with a Christmas message or quotation. Shop-bought decorations were unheard of. People had to be inventive, using what they had around them to create very personal and well-loved family things.

Sue Thompson has designed two beautiful sewing ideas to decorate a mantelpiece and a fireside chair. The cheerful edging could also be used along any shelf or dresser in a kitchen or dining room. The cushion has many wonderful details. It is made using a square of spotted Viyella fabric, framed with red-and-green tartan fabric. A green felt Christmas tree is appliquéd into place, then gold braid is used to outline the frame and decorate the tree. A sawtooth edging made from felt is used around the cushion.

Sawtoothed green felt is also used to define the triangular points which make up the shelf edging. A fine line of green ribbon runs along the whole width of the edging, with little bows as accents where the points meet. Rosettes of contrasting tartan ribbon highlight each point and are held in place with a small covered button.

Above and overleaf: An old-fashioned idea which is well worth reviving is a decorative and cheerful fabric edging to hang jauntily along a shelf or above a fireplace.
Right: A very special Christmas heirloom to lovingly stitch during the months before the festivities. It contains masses of very unusual and pretty details, challenging enough for an experienced needlewoman, yet it is still simple enough for most people to copy from the instructions.

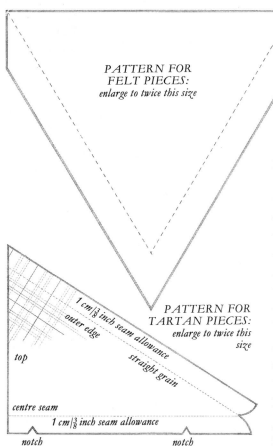

PATTERN FOR FELT PIECES: enlarge to twice this size

1 cm/⅜ inch seam allowance

outer edge

top

straight grain

centre seam

1 cm/⅜ inch seam allowance

notch   *notch*

PATTERN FOR TARTAN PIECES: enlarge to twice this size

MANTELPIECE TRIMMING

MATERIALS

scraps of cotton tartan fabric, for triangles and binding

green felt, for triangles

contrasting tartan ribbon, about 2.5 cm/1 inch wide, for rosettes

narrow satin ribbon, about 3 mm/⅛ inch wide, for bows

tiny button forms, for centres of rosettes

TO MAKE

1 For the binding, cut a strip of cotton tartan 9 cm/3½ inches wide by the length required, adding two seam allowances. Press in half lengthwise, and press 1.5 cm/⅝ inch to the wrong side on each long edge.

2 Calculate how many triangles are needed, and cut one in felt for each triangle as shown in diagram, pinking the edges.

3 Cut one pair of triangles in tartan cotton for each triangle, as shown in diagram. Lay each pair with right sides together, matching notches on centre seam, and stitch, back-stitching firmly at pointed end. Open out, and press seam open. Also press seam allowance to wrong side on outer edges, mitring the point neatly.

4 Lay tartan triangles on felt triangles centrally, and pin in place. Stitch across top and close to outer edges.

5 Leaving the seam allowances pressed under, open out the binding. Lay triangles right side up, on binding. Fold binding over triangles, pin and stitch close to edge of binding, turning in ends.

6 Make bows from the narrow ribbon. To make rosettes from tartan ribbon, cut 20 cm/8 inch lengths, join into rings and gather one long edge tightly. Cover button forms with circles of tartan cotton fabric, and stitch in place at centre of rosettes. Stitch bows and rosettes in place on edge of binding.

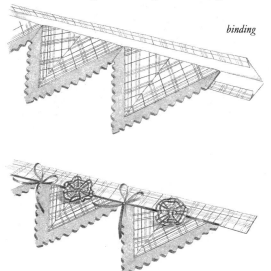

binding

CHRISTMAS TREE CUSHION

MATERIALS

red cotton tartan, for frame

white cotton tartan, for back

CHRISTMAS TREE PATTERN: enlarge to twice this size

black Viyella fabric with white spots, for background

dark green felt, for Christmas tree and cushion edge

transfer fusing web for sticking tree in place and front of cushion to wadding

black-and-gold chevron braid, for trimming the tree

old-gold braid, for inner edge of frame

lightweight Terylene wadding (batting)

35 cm/14 inch zip

embroidery thread in two colours (red and black), such as Clarks Anchor machine embroidery thread

blue star sequins

Russia braid (soutache) in three colours (red, yellow, green), for outer edge

TO MAKE

1 Cut out the four frame pieces as shown in diagram at top of page 69, adding 1.5 cm/⅝ inch seam allowances all around.

2 Stitch the four mitred seams, and press

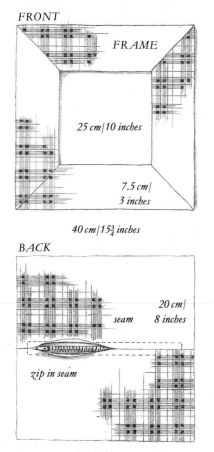

FRONT

FRAME

25 cm/10 inches

7.5 cm/
3 inches

40 cm/15¾ inches

BACK

20 cm/
8 inches

seam

zip in seam

*(These are the finished measurements.
Add 1.5 cm/⅝ inch seam allowances all around.)*

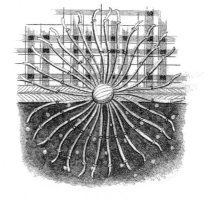

Making the candles

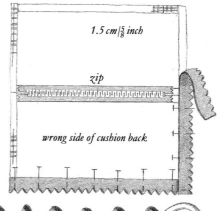

1.5 cm/⅝ inch

zip

wrong side of cushion back

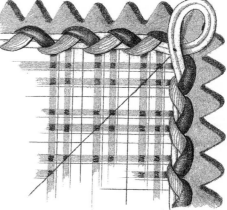

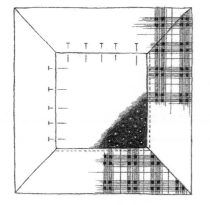

open. Press seam allowances on inner edge of frame to wrong side.

3 Cut out two pieces for cushion back, each 43 × 23 cm/17 × 9¼ inches. Join these along one long edge, leaving a 35 cm/14 inch opening for the zip. Press seam open, and set in zip. Press seam allowances to wrong side.

4 For the background, cut out a piece of spotted fabric 28 cm/11 inches square. Lay frame on it and pin. Stitch all around close to edge of frame, by machine or by hand.

5 Press felt on to fusing web. Cut out Christmas tree from it using pinking shears. Peel

off backing. Press on to spotted background.

6 Cut enough chevron braid for branches plus 6 cm/2½ inches. Pin on tree. Fray gold thread back to end of each branch. Cut off the two 'core' threads close to end of branch. Gather together black threads and twist tightly, bending back under braid. Stitch and trim. Twist gold threads into a rope, pin in place 5 mm/¼ inch above branch and oversew with red thread to form a candle. Twist remaining gold threads loosely, and form into a flame shape, keeping ends tightly together. Oversew end with red thread, and trim gold threads to

2 mm/1/16 inch above stitches. Stitch down flame threads at intervals.

7 Stitch chevron braid branches in place.

8 Pin old-gold braid around inner edge of frame. Cut off, leaving an extra 10 cm/4 inches on each end. Arrange join to be above point of tree. Fray gold threads back at each end to correct length, and knot core threads together. Trim core threads to knot.

9 Use some of the gold threads to sew over knot to hide it. Spread out remaining gold threads to form a star; catch-stitch in place.

10 Cut pieces of fusing web to fit framed panel without seam allowances. Iron fusing web on

to wrong side. Peel off backing. Lay panel on wadding and press, from right side, using a damp cloth. Sew sequins on each side of tree. Press seam allowances over wadding.

11 Cut 4 strips of felt 3 × 44 cm/1¼ × 17 inches, pinking one long edge of each. Lay on edges of zipped back, with pinked edges overlapping cushion edges. Pin, lapping ends. Stick together with fusing web. Trim away excess back.

12 Pin panel to back, wrong sides together, so felt edge sticks out evenly all around. Machine all around close to edge of tartan.

13 Pin yellow braid around edge, forming loops at corners. Sew with tiny back-stitches 1 cm/⅜ inches apart. Thread red and green braid in and out of spaces between stitches.

TAPESTRY TREE DECORATIONS

Few people would know how to blow a glass bauble to decorate a Christmas tree, but it is perfectly possible to build up a collection of hand-made tree decorations which will last for a lifetime. Chris Timms has designed a set of six hanging tapestry shapes, each with a different picture but all with subtle harmonizing colours. The fronts are worked in cross-stitch and the backs are plain matching felt. Although small, each will take several hours or more to make—a perfect project for the winter evenings leading up to Christmas.

The decorations are worked on evenweave fabric of different counts— 14, 18 and 22. All six can be made as a set. Alternatively, if you have little time or experience, or if you find the small stitch hard on your eyes, you could make up the larger (14 count) designs—the goose and the Christmas rose. Once you have tried a few of these, there should be nothing to prevent you from creating your own designs. You could make one for each child in the family, perhaps incorporating initials, names or favourite toys. Muted, old-fashioned thread colours give a nostalgic, faded, Victorian look, while bold, clashing primary colours and metallic threads look bright and modern. These decorations were made using matt stranded cotton but shiny mercerized cotton or silk thread would produce stunning effects.

Take care piecing the shapes together and padding them. The finishing will make all the difference to the final result.

Full instructions are given on page 74.

Above and right: Tiny stitches in soft coloured threads edged with a fine gold cord make tree decorations destined to become well-loved family heirlooms.

DVLCE IVD

A TREASURE CHEST

A glowing, magical, lapis and gold trunk filled with surprises seems to be the stuff of fairy tales. This medieval inspired painted chest holds the treasures for another perfect Christmas. An old wooden box, past its prime, was decorated and gilded and trimmed with braids by designer Kevin McCloud. Lined inside with new paper, it is big enough to hold tree decorations and all the Christmas paraphernalia that a household is likely to collect over the years.

As well as being beautifully decorative in its own right, the box is a very practical storage solution for the mass of stuff which accumulates during the festive season. Keep it shut away out of sight in an attic or spare room, and make a kind of ritual of bringing it downstairs whenever the celebrations begin before Christmas. Once the box is emptied it can remain on show, providing temporary storage for gifts or wrapping paper, ribbons, scissors and labels. On Twelfth Night, fill the box again with all the Christmas bits and pieces, and store it away for the rest of the year.

The decorations on the box look complicated but are very easy to copy from the instructions. Powder-paint pigment was used to get a true intensity of colour, and the bands of gold are made with transfer gold leaf. The rows of angels are actually colour photocopies from a reproduction of a painting.

Left and above: A glorious treasure chest waits in the attic. Fill it with decorations and all the special things for the house at Christmas.

MAKING THE TREASURE CHEST

MATERIALS
old wooden box with a lid
oil-based undercoat or shellac
powder pigments in ultramarine and yellow ochre
PVA binder
gold transfer leaf, or gold foil cardboard or paper, or gold powder paint
black Indian ink
colour photocopies of suitable decoration
wallpaper paste
beeswax polish or oil-based varnish
cord, for edging and handles
upholsterers' large-headed tacks
wallpaper to line inside of box

TO MAKE
1 Wash and clean the box, and sand down the surface in order to key it. Do not fill holes or defects—leave them to give an aged look. Drill four holes, two each side, to take cord later for handles.
2 Paint outside of box with a base coat of oil-based undercoat or thinned shellac. Paint two or three coats of pure ultramarine powder pigment mixed with PVA binder thinned down with water, letting each coat dry. Finish with a coat of PVA binder to seal.
3 Paint a strip of yellow ochre pigment mixed with PVA binder as a base for the gold leaf. If you have experience of oil-gilding, you could oil-gild the strip as on the chest in the photograph. Otherwise simply glue gold foil cardboard or paper in place, or paint with gold powder paint. Leave to harden.
4 Choose a relevant quote such as *In Dulci Jubilo* to paint on in black Indian ink. Trace a Celtic-style typeface, or any which seems suitable, in pencil and fill in with a brush.
5 Colour photocopy the picture you have

chosen. Cut out and glue the paper shapes in place, using wallpaper paste. Overlap where necessary to get a good pattern repeat. Brush the paste on lavishly, front and back. When they are in position, wipe away excess paste from front of paper.
6 When they are very dry, coat with two coats of PVA binder thinned with water (1 part PVA to 2 parts water) to seal the paper well.
7 Paint on extra stars and other suitable motifs in yellow ochre, spreading them quite randomly across the top and sides of the box. Gild over them or paint with gold paint.
8 Leave the painted box to harden for about a week. Polish with a coat of beeswax, or varnish with an oil-based varnish. Using a glue gun and starting at a back edge, fix cord to top edge of box. When cord is in place, hammer in decorative pins at regular spacing.
9 To make the handles, plait (braid) three strands of cord and thread into holes. Glue loose ends and press back against walls of box. Hammer in large-headed tacks to each strand and add more glue to give a very secure fixing. Line the inside of the box with wallpaper, covering over the handles.

MAKING THE TREE DECORATIONS

MATERIALS
3 squares of felt to match the background colour of the designs
Aida cloth 14 count
28 × 32 cm/11¼ × 12¾ inches
Aida cloth 18 count
28 × 32 cm/11¼ × 12¾ inches
Aida cloth 22 count
28 × 32 cm/11¼ × 12¾ inches
.25 metre/⅓ yard of 1 cm/⅜ inch-thick wadding (batting)
1 packet of size 18–24 tapestry needles
2 metres/2¼ yards of 2 mm/⅛ inch-wide gold braid

For the whole set you will need 33 skeins of DMC stranded embroidery cotton (6 strands) in colours: white, grey 451, dark grey 535, pink 948, light grey 648, dark green 924, red 347, dark blue 824, dark brown 3021, pale pink 225, green 500, green 501, pink 224, light blue 931, gold 676, lilac 3042, lilac 3041, light grey 648, light blue 928, light brown 839, deep pink 223, pink 928, rust 221, light rust 356, light green 503, grey 414, light brown 840, gold 977, light green 504, green 927, green 926, green 3052, green 522.
(For part sets please refer to colours on individual design keys.)

NOTE: To make the patterns easier to follow, enlarge them on a photocopier. Leave a good 4 cm/1½ inches of unworked fabric on each side and top and bottom of the design. Make sure the beginning and end of the thread are well secured. The uppermost stitch of the cross should always be in the same direction; this makes the surface look smoother. Two strands of the cotton are used for embroidery on the 18 and 22 count cloth, and three strands are used for the 14 count cloth. It is easier to embroider the design first and fill in the surrounding colour when the design is completed.

TO MAKE
1 With the needle threaded with two (or three) strands of the first colour (refer to chart) and using cross stitch, insert the needle from the back to the front side of the fabric, leaving a short (1.5 cm/⅝ inch) end of thread at the back of the cloth which you sew over with the first few stitches. Make sure it is firm before continuing. Do not use a knot or the lump will show.
2 When you come to the end of the thread, pass it through to the back of the fabric, thread it under the last few stitches and over-sew securely. Cut the end neatly.
3 When you start the next new thread, run the threaded needle under several of the last completed stitches then oversew it securely

GOOSE
(14 count)
- ☐ *white*
- ◨ *light grey 648*
- ◪ *dark green 924*
- ◪ *grey 451*
- ⊠ *dark grey 535*
- ⊟ *orange 356*

SKATERS
(22 count)
- ◺ *dark brown 3021*
- ◪ *lilac 3041*
- ⊤ *deep pink 223*
- ◪ *dark green 924*
- ⊡ *dark blue 824*
- ⊞ *pale pink 225*
- ⊟ *pink 948*
- ◥ *rust 221*
- ⊠ *light rust 356*
- ◖ *light green 503*
- ◥ *grey 414*
- ☐ *light brown 840*
- ◩ *gold 977*
- ◥ *red 347*
- ☐ *white*

GIRL
(22 count)
- ☐ *white*
- ◥ *red 347*
- ⊡ *dark blue 824*
- ◪ *dark brown 3021*
- ⊞ *pale pink 225*
- ◪ *green 500*
- ◪ *green 501*
- ◱ *pink 224*
- ◣ *light blue 931*

...STMAS
...E (14 count)
- *...ht green 504*
- *...en 927*
- *...en 926*
- *...rk green 924*
- *...ht green 928*
- *...en 3052*
- *...en 522*
- *...y 648*
- *...ite*
- *...ak*
- *...4*

...E
(...unt)
- *...d 347* · *lilac 3042*
- *...en 500* ◪ *lilac 3041*
- *...en 501* ☐ *white*
- *...d 676* ◺ *brown 3021*

ANGEL (18 count)
- ☐ *pink 225*
- ◰ *pink 224*
- ⊙ *dark blue 824*
- ◖ *light grey 648*
- ⊟ *pink 948*
- ◙ *lilac 3042*
- ◩ *light blue 928*
- ⊠ *light brown 839*
- ◪ *dark brown 3021*

through the back of the last stitch before continuing. Follow chart for when to change colour.

4 When working horizontally it is easier to do a row of the underneath arms of the cross in one direction, and then cross them on the way back. When working vertically, or diagonally, you may find it easier to cross the stitches as you go.

5 When the design is completed, trace around the outside edge of the embroidery on tracing paper. Cut out the shape to use as a template for the felt. Cut it out very slightly larger than the line.

6 Using the same paper template, cut out two pieces of wadding (batting) for each design. Cut around the embroidery design following the line of the outside edge leaving 2½–3 cm/1–1¼ inches of unworked fabric all around the design. Place embroidery face downwards on a flat surface and place two pieces of wadding in position over the design. Fold the unworked cloth back over the wadding and hand-sew together.

7 Place piece of cut-out felt over the back. Oversew the edges with small stitches.

8 Starting at the bottom of the design, place the gold braid over the edge stitching. Do three or four stitches to hold it in place across the end of the braid, as the end has a tendency to split if sewn through. Sew the braid on over the felt and embroidery join with small oversewing stitches on the front side first. When you get to the centre top of the design form a loop with 10 cm/4 inches of braid, sewing the ends of the loop together securely, because that is where the strain will occur when it is placed on the tree. Continue sewing the braid around the decoration until you reach the start again. Cut off the braid with approximately 1½ cm/⅝ inch overlap. Turn the end under and oversew along both sides and the folded-under end, pulling the thread down as tightly as possible so that the join looks neat. Complete the decoration by oversewing the braid all around on the back (felt side).

CHAPTER 5

FESTIVE
FEASTS

Winter celebrations, whether pagan or religious, have always concentrated on food. Winter was a difficult and lean time centuries ago, but store cupboards were plundered and cellars raided to make special meals that would mark the important occasion.

Every meal eaten during the Christmas festivities has a celebratory feel whether it is a late lazy breakfast with the family at the kitchen table, or a joyful gathering of friends dressed in their party best. Winter foods are warming and welcoming, richly coloured and enticingly fragrant as if to suit the Christmas traditions of plenty and feasting.

Today, we continue to cook food in traditional ways, with ingredients we might not use during the rest of the year. We relive Christmases past with family dishes handed down for generations, though we have now often adapted recipes to make them lighter and less cloying. Certain elements crop up time and time again in Christmas recipes. Spices, dried fruits and nuts are particularly important and wines and spirits are often used for Christmas cooking. The focus has always been on one elaborate and very special meal, usually eaten on Christmas Day but in some countries on Christmas Eve. More often than not this meal is based around a splendid roast goose or turkey.

But these days, anything goes, so long as it is special and different enough from more humdrum daily meals. Every cook takes particular care at this time of year and is prepared to spend longer in the kitchen. Often the food preparations are one of the best parts of the slow build-up to the great day. The sense of pleasure from filling the larder with food to please family and friends is immense. It gives a glow of satisfaction like storing enough logs to feed the fire for a few days, or gathering evergreen boughs to decorate the house.

In this chapter Philippa Davenport, Country Living's award-winning cookery editor, adds her characteristically inventive touch to recipes in the age-old tradition of country hospitality.

PARTRIDGE IN THE VINE

Vine leaves have a long and honourable history in the English kitchen. Tudor and Stuart cooks stewed them with fruit, and Hannah Glasse recommended vine-leaf fritters, but vine leaves were most often used—as here—to wrap and seal in the juices of delicately flavoured meats during cooking. The use of grapes and grape juice is a natural extension of the gentle fruity theme and nicely complements the subtle taste of partridge. *Serves 4–8.*

4 plump young partridge
50 g/2 oz butter and a little olive oil
4 large rashers (slices) streaky bacon
1 or 2 vine leaves per bird, or cabbage leaves if vine leaves are unobtainable
4–8 large, thick rounds of bread
1–2 bunches of watercress
175 ml/6 fl oz unsweetened white grape juice
75 g/3 oz white grapes per person, preferably muscatel

If using fresh vine leaves, make them pliable by blanching. Drop them into a pan of fast-boiling water; cook for 1–1½ min, drain well and pat dry with kitchen paper towels. If using brined vine leaves, soak, rinse and dry them carefully following instructions on the packet or tin. Cabbage leaves may not be as romantic but they are a good and practical alternative. Choose the large, outer leaves of a firm green-leafed cabbage such as Savoy, and blanch them, as described for fresh vine leaves, to make them easier to use for wrapping.

Put a hazelnut-sized knob of well seasoned butter into the body cavity of each bird and rub the skin all over with salt and freshly ground black pepper. Cut the bacon rashers in half if long. Cover the breasts of the birds with the bacon, then encase each bird completely in a neat wrapping of leaves and tie them securely with string.

To prepare the grapes it is necessary only to halve and seed them. I have tried this recipe using grapes which have been peeled as well as halved and seeded, and concluded that the extra effort involved was not justified—unless the grapes have unusually coarse thick skins. Flute the rounds of bread prettily, fry them lightly in best-quality olive oil, drain well and keep them hot.

To cook the partridge, first lay the birds breast down on a rack in a roasting tin. Melt the remaining butter and pour it over them. Roast at 220°C/425°F/mark 7 for 15 min. Baste the birds thoroughly with the buttery pan juices, turn them breast up and roast for 15 min more. Then unparcel the birds, removing vine leaves and bacon wrappings. Baste the birds well with the pan juices and continue roasting for a further 5–6 min, breast up, until the skin is pale golden brown. Tilt the birds to let the juices run from the body cavities back into the roasting pan. Transfer the birds on to a warmed serving dish, placing each one on a round of hot fried bread (or halve the birds first if serving one between two people) and put to rest in a warm place for 15 minutes or so before serving.

Skim some of the fat from the roasting pan. Add the grapes and the grape juice to the pan and shake to swirl and moisten the grapes. Put the pan into the switched-off oven (or place it directly over a very low heat) for a few minutes to warm and slightly soften the fruit. Lift the grapes out of the pan with a slotted spoon, pile them round the birds and garnish with a big clump of watercress. Season the grape-juice gravy remaining in the pan with salt and pepper to taste, and transfer to a warmed sauce boat. A few game chips or potato sticks are the only other accompaniment that is necessary.

Left:
Partridge in
the Vine.
Overleaf:
Chrysanthemum
Duck.

CHRYSANTHEMUM DUCK

With its glorious glaze and the bitter-sweet fragrance of the accompanying salad, this makes a sensational alternative to classic crispy roast duck. No problems about carving—duck joints are used. Just add or subtract to cater for larger or smaller parties. *Serves 6.*

6 large duck joints (quarters)
fresh root ginger
5 small thin-skinned oranges
a little runny honey, soy sauce and olive oil
1–2 large chrysanthemums, preferably tawny gold
watercress or chicory
a few unsalted cashew nuts, toasted under the grill

Remove any lumps of excess fat from the duck joints (quarters), and prick the skin all over with a fork, angling it carefully to avoid piercing deep into the flesh or precious meat juices as well as fat will run out during cooking.

Peel and chop very finely indeed 2 generous tablespoons fresh root ginger. Lay the duck joints in a dish and rub them all over with the chopped ginger and a good grinding of pepper, but no salt. Pour on 30 ml/2 tablespoons juice freshly squeezed from one orange. Turn the meat several times to moisten it all over. Cover and set aside in a cool place for several hours, preferably overnight, so the duck absorbs some of the flavours.

Drain the marinade from the duck and scrape off the ginger. Reserve this and the marinade liquid. Put the duck joints, skin side up, on to a rack in a baking dish or roasting tin and roast in an oven heated to 200°C/400°F/mark 6 for 45 minutes. (If the duck joints are very large and your oven is quite small you may need to use two dishes and two racks—and swap oven positions half-way through cooking.)

Stand the honey jar in a bowl of hot water for 10 minutes so that the honey becomes runny enough to measure easily. Mix 30 ml/2 tbsp of the honey with the orange and ginger marinade mixture, then stir in 10 ml/2 tsp soy sauce plus a pinch of salt to make an aromatic glaze. Pour off the duck fat that has collected in the roasting tin—save it for frying. Brush the glaze all over the flesh and skin of the duck and continue roasting, still with skin side up and still on the rack, for another 20 minutes. Baste once during this time, making sure that all the little pieces of ginger adhere to the duck skin. By the end of the cooking time the meat should be well cooked yet succulent and the skin should be burnished to a rich mahogany-coloured glaze. If the duck looks in danger of burning, cover the dish with a dome of foil. More probably it will be necessary to cover only the wing tips or drumsticks—the parts which are most prone to burning.

To make the accompanying salad, first peel 3–4 small thin-skinned oranges. Use a very sharp knife and be ruthless about cutting away every trace of the bitter white pith. Slice the oranges across into thin rounds, sprinkle them with a little pepper, a scrunch of sea-salt and a drizzle of oil. Arrange them prettily in a shallow dish. Add a few nuts if you wish and a scant handful of chicory leaves or watercress sprigs, but bear in mind that the salad should be composed mainly of orange and chrysanthemum.

Immediately before serving, sprinkle the salad with another spoonful of oil and a squeeze of orange, then quickly pile the fresh chrysanthemum petals on top. The slightly bitter fragrance of the flowers complements the rich glazed duck beautifully. Huge tawny gold blooms look most dramatic: simply pull the petals from the flower-heads, tugging them gently, a small handful at a time, so they do not become bruised or spoiled.

GOOSE WITH RABBIT, LEMON AND PARSLEY

A goose will not feed a large family generously, hence the farmhouse tradition of roasting the bird with a rabbit inside it. The rabbit absorbs some of the goose flavour as it cooks and used to be served to the women and children, leaving more goose for the men! I do things rather differently. I bone several rabbits and pack them with plenty of fragrant stuffing inside a boned-out goose. The result is a magnificent roast, rich and succulent, that will easily serve 12 or more people—and everyone gets a fair share of the bird. It is delicious served hot, although the stuffing tends to crumble and fall untidily from the slices, and excellent cold, when it seems impossible not to carve impeccably. Use a fresh bird, not frozen, and don't be daunted by the idea of boning it. Small birds are fiddly; goose is easy but it does take time.

a plump, fresh goose with an oven-ready weight of about 4.3 kg/9½ lb (I don't recommend a bird of less than 4 kg/9 lb or more than 4.4 kg/9¾ lb for this recipe)
3 wild rabbits weighing about 1 kg/2½ lb each in the fur (enough to yield a total of 1 kg/2½ lb filleted meat)
zest of 4 lemons and 60 ml/4 tbsp lemon juice
75 g/3 oz chopped parsley and 15 ml/1 tbsp fresh thyme
350 g/12 oz fresh breadcrumbs and 75 g/3 oz butter

Remove the fat from the tail end of the bird and render it down. Cut off the legs at the knuckle end of the drumstick and cut off the wing pinions. Lay the bird on its breast and cut through the skin and the flesh to the backbone from the parson's nose to the neck. Then cut and scrape the flesh from the carcass with a small sharp knife held close to the bone. Free the fleshy 'oysters' carefully and work down each side of the bird, exposing the rib cage. When you get to the tip of the breast cut through the cartilage. Cut through the wings where they join the carcass then pare the flesh free from the wing bones, working from the carcass end towards the tips. Free the leg meat in similar fashion, first cutting through the socket joints that attach the legs to the carcass, then scraping the meat clean from the thigh and drumstick bones.

Skin the rabbits and strip the meat from the bones, keeping the chunks as large as possible. Weigh out 1 kg/2½ lb for this recipe. Use the rabbit and goose bones, giblets, neck and other trimmings to make a rich stock which can be served as gravy.

To make the stuffing, first warm the butter with an equal weight of melted goose fat in a largish pan. Away from the heat, add the lemon juice and zest, the herbs and bread-crumbs. Season generously and cool.

Lay the boned bird skin-side down. Spread half the stuffing over the central area of the flesh. Put the rabbit fillets on top, season well and sprinkle the rest of the stuffing over and around them to fill in the gaps and make an even mound. Bring up the sides of the bird over the filling, as though wrapping a parcel. Aim for a plump pillow, but one that is not too tightly packed as the stuffing will swell during roasting.

Using fine string or strong button cotton (thread), firm stitches and a good overlap, sew the bird up from neck to tail end. Then sew it across the vent, and at the neck. Tuck in the leg and wing flesh, like pockets, and sew down the folds neatly. Finally, check the skin for any nicks and tears and patch them tidily. Then weigh the stuffed bird so you can calculate cooking time. The bird is now ready to roast or (more convenient I find) it can be covered loosely and stored in a cold larder or in a refrigerator overnight—but be sure to bring the bird back to normal room temperature

two hours or so before you need to cook it.

To cook, rub the goose skin all over with salt and pepper. Lay the bird breast-down on a rack in a roasting pan and drape it with a double thickness of butter-muslin soaked in melted goose fat. Roast at 220°C/425°F/mark 7 for 15 minutes, then at 180°C/350°F/mark 4 for 1 hour 20 minutes to 1½ hours depending on whether the weight of the stuffed bird was a little under or over 4.5 kg/10 lb. Check periodically that the butter-muslin is moist, and pour off the surplus fat.

Turn the bird breast-up and continue roasting, at the same temperature and still cloaked in fat-soaked butter-muslin, for a further 45

minutes. Finally, remove the butter-muslin and pour off all the fat that has collected in the pan. Turn the temperature up to 220°C/425°F/mark 7 and fast-roast for 15 minutes to crisp the breast skin a little.

If the goose is to be eaten hot, let the cooked bird rest for 30 minutes before carving. Floury potatoes, clear gravy and red cabbage cooked with spices and sautéed dessert apple go well with hot goose cooked by this method.

Above: Goose with Rabbit, Lemon and Parsley.
Overleaf: Dukka is served with warm French bread and best olive oil.

FROZEN PLUM PUDDING

The rich and heavy mixtures that go into Christmas cake and the usual plum pudding are so alike that to serve both on the same day seems repetitive. The alternative Christmas pudding given here is much lighter and fresher, and its frosty white looks are a delight. The good news for the cook is that, unlike traditional steamed plum pudding, this one does not need to be made weeks or months ahead—Christmas week is soon enough—and the method is blissfully easy. For memorably good results use whole candied peel, fresh nuts and top-quality fruits, *not* anonymous 'dried fruit cake and pudding mixture'. Crown the pudding with a sprig of frosted holly and serve it alone for delicious purity. Or accompany it with a fruity sauce. **Serves 12.**

---

25 g/1 oz each pitted prunes, dried apricots, glacé (candied) cherries, sultanas (golden raisins), currants, candied whole peel, walnuts, hazelnuts (filberts) and flaked almonds

50 g/2 oz raisins and 2 oranges

a little brandy, allspice and cinnamon

300 ml/10 fl oz each double (heavy) cream and whipping cream

3 egg whites and 45 ml/3 tbsp caster (superfine) sugar

Chop the large fruits into smaller pieces, mix them with 2.5 ml/$\frac{1}{2}$ tsp each ground allspice and cinnamon and the finely grated zest of the oranges. Pour on the juice of the oranges and 45 ml/3 tbsp cheap brandy. Chop the walnuts and hazelnuts (filberts) and sprinkle them over the fruits together with the flaked almonds— do not stir the nuts into the fruits. Cover and leave in a cool place for about eight hours. Meanwhile chill in the freezer a pudding basin, round Christmas pudding mould, or ice cream bombe mould of 1.5 litres/2$\frac{3}{4}$ pint capacity

(alternatively you could chill several smaller containers).

Gently stir the macerated fruits and nuts together and tip them into a sieve placed over a bowl to catch the juices. Add both sorts of cream to the juices and whip, then fold the fruit and nut mixture into the whipped cream. Whisk the egg whites in a separate bowl, gradually whisking in the caster sugar to make a meringue mixture, then fold the meringue into the cream. Spoon the mixture into the chilled mould, taking care to fill the corners smoothly. Cover with a double thickness of foil and freeze for about 10 hours.

This is a very soft-textured ice-cream and therefore very easy to unmould. Unmould it on to a well-chilled plate before the meal begins, and return it to the freezer with the inverted pudding basin over it. Serve Frozen Plum Pudding straight from the freezer, quickly unveiling it and crowning it with a sprig of sugar-frosted holly before you bring it to the table.

CRANBERRY AND POMEGRANATE JELLY

Cranberries have escaped from their usual role of saucing the turkey to partner pomegranates in this light and fragrant confection, which would make a fine finale for a special meal. If fresh pomegranates are difficult to buy in your area, I suggest you search out a bottle of grenadine syrup instead. This highly sweetened concentrate of pomegranate juice is much used in cooking and for drinks in France, and is stocked by discerning delicatessens and wine merchants. Very little is needed for this recipe but grenadine keeps well and I am sure you will find it popular for drinks, particularly with children. Dilute it with mineral or soda water and serve it on crushed ice with plenty of lemon juice for a strictly non-alcoholic and very sweet variation on Campari and soda. **Serves 6–8.**

---

350 g/12 oz fresh cranberries

2 pomegranates (or 45 ml/3 tbsp grenadine syrup diluted in 135 ml/9 tbsp water)

sugar, gelatine powder and rose water

Cut the pomegranates in half, scoop out the seeds and discard the bitter-tasting strands of yellow pith that divide them. Reserve 30–45 ml/2 or 3 tbsp of the most brilliantly coloured whole seeds for garnish, wrapping them in clingfilm (plastic wrap) to keep them fresh. Put the rest into a piece of butter-muslin, twist it tightly, hold it over a bowl or measuring jug and squeeze hard with your hands to extract as much juice as possible. Sprinkle on to the juices 12.5 ml/2$\frac{1}{2}$ tsp gelatine powder and set aside.

Simmer the cranberries very gently in 500 ml/16 fl oz of water in a tightly covered pan. Crush the cooked fruit lightly with a potato masher, then tip the contents of the pan into a sieve suspended over a bowl containing 75 g/3 oz sugar. Leave to drip for 30 min.

Warm the gelatine and pomegranate mixture gently until the gelatine is dissolved and the liquid is clear, then stir this into the cranberry juices. Measure the combined liquids and add cold water if necessary to make up to 750 ml/24 fl oz in total. Stir in a *soupçon* of triple-distilled rose water to heighten the aroma, divide between small glasses—cocktail or syllabub glasses are ideal—and chill until set to a soft tremulous jelly.

I like this best simply served with the reserved pomegranate seeds sprinkled over the top—a decorative clue to the ingredients of the jelly— but you may like to add small snowy billows of *crème fraîche*.

DUKKA

I first tasted Dukka with friends in Cairo, and I rate it as the best of all nibbles to serve with drinks. My friends seem to find it irresistible too, so I like to keep some permanently at the ready in my store cupboard. It is useful all year round and invaluable at this most social time of year when the country woman's reputation for hospitality is truly put to the test. **Makes about 175 g/6 oz.**

---

100 g/4 oz hazelnut (filbert) kernels and 50 g/2 oz sesame seeds

25 g/1 oz coriander seeds and 30 ml/2 tbsp cumin seeds

Warm a frying pan over medium heat (without any fat). Add the hazels and cook, stirring and turning them until the skins begin to blacken and peel, and can be blown away. Empty the pan and reduce heat to low. Lightly toast the sesame seeds until pale golden, then warm the coriander and cumin seeds together until crisp and aromatic.

Mix all four ingredients together with some sea salt and black pepper and crush coarsely, using the largest blade of a meat mincer. (Don't use a blender or food-processor; it will reduce at least some of the ingredients to a fine powder.) Check seasoning and if not for immediate use, store in an airtight jar. Dukka keeps for several weeks but it is best when toasty and crisp. If it has been made some time ago, spread it on a baking tray and heat it briefly in a moderate oven before serving.

Serve Dukka with warm French bread and a small bowl of good olive oil. To eat, break off a small piece of bread. Holding it by the crust, dip the crumb into the oil, moistening it well, then press into the spiced nutty mixture.

ORANGE SALAD

A simple dish of oranges sliced into rings is transformed by the addition of splinters of homemade hazelnut (filbert) praline aromatized with a few finely ground cardamom seeds. Re-form the sliced oranges, securing with wooden cocktail sticks. Pile into a pyramid and scatter the hazelnut praline over them.

Above: Orange Salad with its cardamom-scented hazelnut praline.
Overleaf: Cranberry and Pomegranate Jelly, and Frozen Plum Pudding.

SPICY THINS

Few bakes could be quicker or easier than these little biscuits, which I make using the American 'refrigerator cookie' method. Make the dough now and bake when needed. Crisp, buttery and capable of being flavoured with various spices, they are a life saver in so many ways: just right for pleasing unexpected visitors at teatime, an elegant choice to serve with syllabubs and other special desserts, and charming when threaded with ribbons to hang on the Christmas tree. ***Makes about 7 dozen.***

---

225 g/8 oz plain white flour and 175 g/6 oz softened butter

100 g/4 oz caster sugar and 25 g/1 oz plus 2.5 ml/½ tsp granulated sugar

spice, citrus juice and zest (see notes below)

Using a spice/coffee mill whizz 25 g/1 oz granulated sugar and the citrus zest to a fragrant powder. Tip it into a food processor. Add the other ingredients, dribbling on the fruit juice last, and mix to a dough. Turn the mixture out and roll it into a sausage shape 4–5 cm/1½–2 inches in diameter and 20–23 cm/8–9 inches long. Sprinkle with 2.5 ml/½ tsp granulated sugar, wrap in greaseproof paper (waxed paper) and refrigerate until very hard (or freeze for long-term storage).

To bake, first heat the oven. When the temperature reaches 190°C/375°F/mark 5, take the biscuit mix from the fridge and shave off 10–15 slices, allowing 8–10 slices per inch. Lay them, well apart, on a lightly oiled or non-stick baking tray and bake for 6–8 minutes, turning the tray once. If the biscuits are to be threaded on to ribbons, make a small hole in each with the tip of a skewer as soon as they emerge from the oven. Quickly loosen them all with a palette knife then lift them one by one on to a cooling rack.

The trick is to bake in small batches (just 15 plain or 10 biscuits with holes at a time) and to know your oven. Test until you get the timing right: the biscuits should be crisp not doughy, and golden or lightly browned.

Allspice version: 5 ml/1 tsp ground allspice, 15 ml/1 tbsp orange juice and the zest of an orange.

Ginger version: 10–15 ml/2–3 tsp ground ginger, 15 ml/1 tbsp lemon juice and the zest of a lemon.

Cinnamon version: 5 ml/1 tsp ground cinnamon, 5 ml/1 tsp lemon juice, 10 ml/2 tsp orange juice and a good pinch of orange zest.

CHRISTMAS MULL

Mulled wine and mince pies sum up the spirit of carol-singing Christmas Eve parties for me. Mid November is not too soon to make the syrup base for mulled wine. It keeps well for several weeks and means one less thing to do when Christmas week frenzy gets under way.

---

juice and zest of 2 oranges and 2 lemons

15–18 cloves and 3 cinnamon sticks, bruised

quarter of a nutmeg, grated and 225 g/8 oz sugar

robust, modestly priced red wine

Spanish brandy (optional)

Put the sugar, spices and citrus fruits into a stainless steel pan. Add 600 ml/1 pt (2½ cups) water, bring to the boil, cover and simmer for 30 min. Set aside until cold then strain through butter-muslin. Bottle and store in a cold larder or fridge if not for immediate use.

To serve, bring some or all of the syrup to the boil. Add red wine (I allow one bottle of wine per 150 ml/5 fl oz spicy syrup) and bring quickly to a bare simmer. On no account boil. Serve in warmed glasses, as is, or add a splash of brandy for extra oomph or dilute with boiling water to taste.

ALMOND SWEETMEATS

A ritzy and aromatic alternative to the ubiquitous chocolate truffles, these would make a lovely last-minute Christmas present for sweet-toothed friends. Wrap the gift prettily and label it with an eat-by date and instructions to store in the fridge. ***Makes 3 dozen.***

---

125 g/4 oz freshly ground almonds and a few flaked almonds

125 g/4 oz unsalted butter, diced, and 175 g/6 oz sugar

the seeds from a few green or white cardamom pods, crushed to a coarse powder

10 ml/2 tsp triple-distilled orange-blossom water

Line a shallow 15 cm/6 inch square baking tin with lightly oiled greaseproof paper (waxed paper). Put the sugar, orange-blossom water and 60 ml/4 tbsp cold water into a pan and heat gently until the sugar dissolves, then boil to the softball stage, when the temperature on a sugar thermometer will reach 113°C/235°F. Away from the heat, quickly add the ground almonds, cardamom and butter and stir to mix well. Turn the mixture into the prepared tin, press it well into the corners and level the top. Score lightly to make 2.5 cm/1 inch squares and press a flaked almond on top of each. Cover and refrigerate for 2 hours or until the mixture is solid.

Turn out the sweetmeats, peel away the paper and cut into squares. Wrap and store them in an airtight container in the fridge, where they will keep for a week—if you can resist eating them for that long.

Right: Three recipes which exploit the delicious scents and flavours of spices. Christmas Mull is an essential Christmas drink; Almond Sweetmeats and Spicy Thins are luxurious extras to have stored away for visitors.

CHAPTER 6

CHRISTMAS IN THE COUNTRY

Families everywhere celebrate Christmas in time-honoured ways. Yet every household also develops its own individual traditions which make the time special. Elisabeth Luard has collected the favourite recipes of a family living in the deepest countryside; here is how they celebrate this most joyous of holidays. Graham Smith-Moorhouse, a country doctor, lives with his wife Gill and two sons James and Rupert in a sheep farming area. There's a lot of hard work in a family Christmas but Gill has become selective over the years about menus and activities, to give everyone a chance to enjoy the season.

Tried-and-tested favourite recipes form the basis of their Christmas menu. They do not have a first course, as they have found it's just too much. Gill's main course takes two hours in the kitchen, from tying on the apron to triumphant dishing up. All offers of assistance are gratefully accepted and directed to peeling and slicing. The family usually has game—a brace of pheasants, or wild duck, or even a wild goose. Instead of stuffing they have a herby Yorkshire pudding, which the men are actively encouraged to make. The game and herby Yorkshire pudding are accompanied by roast potatoes, Brussels sprouts, a good gravy, and cranberry sauce. The Christmas pudding follows, which Gill has usually started cooking late in the afternoon. With this there is a choice of brandy butter, rum sauce or double cream. There is coffee and port or brandy to finish. This meal is eaten on Christmas Eve. Food for Christmas Day is more casual, with leftovers of meat and salad accompanied by homemade pickled onions, red cabbage and chutney, and perhaps hot mince pies and cream. A large honey-baked ham is cooked and a joint of beef left cold to be thick-cut for sandwiches.

To sustain keen appetites whetted by fresh winter air and outdoor activities, plenty of simple, filling food is required through the Christmas holidays. The ham Gill traditionally cooks at this time of year feeds many people with very little effort. It can be served either with delicious dishes of baked root vegetables, or cold with salads, pickles and chutneys. Whole hams are best managed by being simmered in boiling water, then finished off in the oven to produce a wonderful rich and sticky glaze.

Christmas is very much a family effort. Everything from tree decorations to presents is homemade. Gill is the coordinator, beginning the week before. During that week, as a contrast to the rich and plentiful meals to come, food is kept simple—a lamb stew, for example, or perhaps a thick pea soup with crusty granary bread.

Gill likes to bake treats for Christmas with the children helping. She makes large batches of florentines and macaroons, which keep very well and make lovely small presents for the children to give. The children help make traditional biscuit shapes to hang on the tree. In October Gill prepares Christmas puddings for the following year, storing them in the freezer.

At the same time a cake is made from an old family recipe which works perfectly year after year. The cake is soaked every two weeks while in store with a couple of teaspoons of brandy. The family has great fun deciding how it will be iced and decorated, usually choosing a traditional snow scene with Santa and sleigh atop the white icing. Gill also bakes a less rich Christmas cake in a long loaf tin, leaving it un-iced to be eaten with slices of white crumbly cheese.

Because the main meal is eaten on Christmas Eve, the celebrations are spread out, rather than being concentrated on just one day. Also, it means that Gill can relax with the rest of the family on Christmas Day, opening presents, going to church, having friends in for drinks and mince pies, or going for walks down the local lanes.

Graham's cellar is his pride and joy. A yearly quota of two judiciously selected crates for laying down has given him a storehouse of future delights. To accompany the pheasant Graham simply decants some Beaujolais Nouveau into a narrow-necked open glass jug; the best wine is saved to be enjoyed on its own by the fire.

Above: The children carry presents to neighbours
up the old stone lane from the farm.
Right: Christmas Eve dinner is taken up the hill
to be eaten by candlelight in the 17th century barn
with sheep-farming neighbours and friends.

RED CABBAGE WITH APPLES AND CRAB-APPLE JELLY

Red cabbage is a favourite winter pickle. It's delicious used fresh in this sweet-sour version, which is perfect with game. *Serves 6.*

450 g/1 lb red cabbage
2 large cooking apples
30–45 ml/2–3 tbsp wine vinegar—preferably tarragon
salt and black pepper, to taste
30 ml/2 tbsp crab-apple (or redcurrant) jelly

Shred and wash the cabbage, discarding the central stalk. Put it in a large heavy pan or casserole. Peel and slice the apples and add, together with salt, pepper and vinegar. Bring to the boil, turn the heat down, and cook slowly, covered tightly, for 1½ hours until the cabbage is tender and the cooking liquid well reduced.

If you have too much liquid reduce by boiling fiercely for a few minutes. Stir in the crab-apple jelly to give the cabbage a lovely sheen.

CRAB-APPLE JELLY

Pick over and wash the crab-apples and put them, whole, in a large preserving pan. Cover to ¾ of the volume with water. Bring to the boil. Simmer until the apples are soft and pulpy. Cool. Strain overnight through muslin. Measure the juice and allow 450 g/1 lb granulated sugar to 600 ml/1 pint juice. Return sugar and juice to the pan and bring to the boil, stirring until the sugar melts. Cook at a rolling boil for 15–20 minutes until a teaspoon of jelly begins to set when tested on a cold saucer. Pour the jelly into sterilized glass jars, filling well up. Cover and seal.

SEASON PUDDING

This is a herbed batter pudding. Graham is the pudding expert in the family. Traditionally a spoonful of snow is added to the milk. *Serves 6.*

225 g/8 oz flour
2.5 ml/½ tsp salt
black pepper
5 ml/1 tsp crumbled dried sage
2 medium eggs
150 ml/5 fl oz milk
30 ml/2 tbsp good beef dripping or lard
1 large onion, skinned and finely chopped

Mix the flour, salt, pepper and sage together. Work in the eggs thoroughly with a wooden spoon. Add 300 ml/10 fl oz water to the milk. Gradually beat in enough of the liquid into the flour-and-egg mixture to make the consistency of the batter a bit thinner than a pancake batter. The consistency should be between thick and running-off-the-spoon.

Put the dripping or lard in a square roasting tin and melt it in the oven at 230°C/450°F/mark 8. Add the onion to the hot fat. Turn the heat down to 220°C/425°F/mark 7. (Unseasoned pudding would be cooked at the higher temperature throughout.) When the onion is browned, pour in the batter. Bake the pudding for 45–50 minutes, until well-puffed and golden. Cut into squares and serve with the pheasant.

TRADITIONAL ROAST BEEF

The favourite roast is 5.5 kg/12 lb of sirloin with the fillet underneath, cooked rare and left to go cold. Then it's ready to be sandwiched between hunks of bread spread with beef dripping, sliced onion and cucumber soaked in vinegar. *Serves 24.*

5.5 kg/12 lb sirloin of beef
50 g/2 oz lard or dripping
5 ml/1 tsp mustard powder
salt and pepper, to taste

Wipe the meat and spread on the lard or dripping. Season with mustard powder, salt and pepper.

For rare beef, roast the joint at 180°C/350°F/mark 4 for 3 hours, basting regularly. For the last 30 minutes, turn the oven up to 220°C/425°F/mark 7. Leave to cool.

MUSHY PEA SOUP

A good thick soup is fuel for hungry workers. Presoak the peas and it will be ready in no time. *Serves 4–6.*

450 g/1 lb dried marrowfat peas
1 onion, skinned and diced
1 carrot, peeled and diced
3 sticks celery, diced
1 small parsnip, peeled and diced
25 g/1 oz butter or lard
600 ml/1 pint meat or vegetable stock
300 ml/½ pint milk
salt and pepper, to taste

Soak the peas overnight in cold water. Drain, cover with fresh water and add 2.5 ml/½ teaspoon salt. Cook the peas for about 30 minutes until mushy.

Meanwhile fry the vegetables until soft in the butter or lard. Sieve or liquidize the peas with the stock. Add the vegetables. Stir well and season with salt and pepper. Bring to the boil. Stir in the milk. Taste and adjust the seasoning. Serve with crusty brown bread.

Right: Thick and warming Mushy Pea Soup served scalding hot from a beautiful old blue and white china tureen.

TRADITIONAL CHRISTMAS TREE BISCUITS

This recipe makes a basic, slightly spicy biscuit (cookie). You can adapt it in any number of ways, for example by adding more of one particular spice, or by including the grated rind of lemon or orange. For a chocolate version, replace 25 g/1 oz of the flour with the same amount of cocoa powder. These biscuits are thinner and less chunky than the gingerbread shapes on page 48. The dough is quite easy for children to work with. **Makes about 50 biscuits.**

225 g/8 oz plain (all-purpose) flour
100 g/4 oz butter
100 g/4 oz caster (superfine) sugar
1 standard egg, beaten
5 ml/1 tsp milk
5 ml/1 tsp ground cinnamon
2.5 ml/½ tsp ground nutmeg
pinch of ground cloves

Grease some baking trays. Put the flour, spices, sugar, and butter into a bowl. Rub the butter into the flour and sugar until the mixture resembles fine breadcrumbs. Pour in the egg and milk, and mix to a dough.

Turn out on to a floured board and roll out to 4 mm/⅛ inch. Cut into circles, hearts, or tree or star shapes and lay on to baking sheets.

At this stage you can if you like cut out the holes for threading the ribbon through. This is best done with a sharp metal piping nozzle about 8 mm/⅜ inch in diameter.

Bake in the oven at 180°C/350°F/mark 4 for approximately 15 minutes until lightly browned. Remove from oven and allow to cool slightly before putting biscuits on a wire rack to finish cooling.

Decorate with white or coloured icing if you like when they are completely cold.

If preferred you can cut the holes out just after the biscuits have come out of the oven. Always leave a good margin of biscuit between the hole and the edge.

MACAROONS

Children love making these delicious little almond macaroons, and they are good to give as gifts. **Makes about 24.**

100 g/4 oz ground almonds
175 g/6 oz caster sugar
2 small egg whites, lightly mixed
blanched almond halves
rice paper

Put ground almonds and sugar into a mixing bowl. Add a little egg white at a time, stirring well. Beat well but keep the mixture quite stiff.

Above and right: Delicious Christmas treats—Florentines and Macaroons.

Line 2 baking trays with rice paper. With wet hands roll small balls of the mixture and place well apart on baking trays. Push a half almond on each biscuit.

Bake in the oven at 180°C/350°F/mark 4 for about 15 minutes until the biscuits are just lightly browned.

Remove from oven, cool for a few minutes and pull off tray.

Pack the macaroons into boxes or small glass jars to give as a gift.

FLORENTINES

Home-made Florentines are indescribably delicious and are a perfect Christmas treat. They can be served with coffee after dinner and are also perfect as gifts.

150 g/4 oz butter
75 g/3 oz caster sugar
30 ml/2 tbsp whipped cream
100 g/4 oz shredded blanched almonds
50 g/2 oz good candied peel, chopped
50 g/2 oz glacé cherries (candied cherries), chopped
approximately 175 g/6 oz bitter plain chocolate

Melt butter and sugar then add cream and allow mixture to boil for 1 minute. Add nuts, peel and cherries, stirring all the time. Drop in neat mounds on to a greased baking tray, leaving plenty of room between them, as they will spread. Bake in the oven at 180°C/350°F/mark 4 for about 10 minutes or until golden brown.

Remove from the oven and leave for a few seconds before gently easing them on to a wire rack with a palette knife.

When cold spread the flat sides with melted chocolate and make wavy lines as a decoration with a fork. Pack into boxes or cellophane-wrapped baskets if giving as a present.

BUTTER-ROASTED PHEASANT WITH PORT GRAVY

Pheasants are among the most handsome wild birds. The beautiful plumage of the cock and the soft, muted browns of the hen make an impressive sight when paired in a brace. They have a strong, gamey flavour and are at their best in November and December—just in time for Christmas. Choose a young bird for roasting. Pluck and dress the brace about 5 days after shooting—longer if you like them high. Reserve 6 tail feathers from each bird and note which is which. *Serves 6.*

2 fine fat young pheasants
salt and pepper, to taste
2 butter-papers
For the gravy: 15 ml/1 tbsp flour
600 ml/1 pint vegetable or chicken stock
gravy browning (optional)
1 glass port

Wipe the birds and singe off any small, overlooked feathers over a naked flame. Put them in a roasting tin, breasts up, and sprinkle with salt and pepper. Cover the breasts with butter-paper.

Roast in the oven at 190°C/375°F/mark 5 for 1¼–1½ hours depending on the size of the birds. Remove the butter-paper 15 minutes before the end to allow the skin to brown. Check if the birds are cooked by gently pulling the leg away from the body—when it comes away easily, and the juices run clear, the birds are done.

Transfer them to a hot serving dish and decorate with the appropriate feathers stuck into the rump.

Blend the flour with enough cold water to make a paste and stir in the vegetable stock. Add a little gravy browning if you like dark gravy. Pour the liquid into the roasting tin and bubble up over the heat, scraping in all the dark delicious bits stuck to the pan. Add salt and pepper and the glass of port. Cook, stirring well, until it thickens. Serve separately with the pheasant.

ROAST GOOSE WITH STUFFING

350 g/12 oz apples, peeled, cored and diced
30 ml/2 tbsp rum
225–350 g/8–12 oz fresh breadcrumbs
4–6 chopped fresh sage leaves
15–30 ml/1–2 tbsp ground mace
1 beaten egg or gravy stock
4 kg/9 lb goose
salt and pepper

Pour the rum over the apples and leave to soak for 3–4 hours. Mix with the remaining ingredients for the stuffing and place inside the cavity. Prick the skin of the bird and rub a little salt and pepper over it. Cover the legs with spare fat taken from inside the goose. Wrap it in aluminium foil or baking parchment. Place on a rack, breast side up, in a meat tin. Roast in the oven at 200°C/400°F/mark 6 for 3½ hours (20 minutes per pound, plus 30 minutes). After the first hour turn the goose over so that the back is uppermost, and unwrap the back to let it brown. Pour over the surplus fat. Make sure that the legs are still covered and that the skin is not burning. For the last 30–45 minutes of the cooking time, turn the goose back on to its back and uncover the breast to brown. Pour over the surplus fat, or remove the fat from the tin.

Right: Christmas Loaf, with its traditional accompaniment, local crumbly white cheese. Overleaf: The family's home in the lee of a valley.

CHRISTMAS LOAF

Make this at least 2 weeks ahead and mature in a tin. Serve with a slice of crumbly white cheese. The same mixture makes a fine Christmas cake. *Makes a 4 lb loaf.*

300 g/11 oz self-raising (self-rising) flour
275 g/10 oz soft brown sugar
300 g/11 oz butter
6 eggs
450 g/1 lb currants, sultanas (golden raisins) and raisins
100 g/4 oz glacé (candied) cherries
100 g/4 oz mixed peel
85 ml/3 fl oz sweet sherry
5 ml/1 tsp mixed spice
2.5 ml/½ tsp grated nutmeg
100 g/4 oz ground almonds

Cream the butter and sugar together with a wooden spoon until light and fluffy. Beat in the eggs one by one, adding 15 ml/1 tbsp of the flour if the mixture goes grainy. Fold in the flour and all the rest of the ingredients. Butter a long loaf tin and line with buttered paper. Pour in the mixture. Bake the cake in the oven at 170°C/325°F/mark 3 for about 2 hours, or a little longer, until a skewer inserted in the centre comes out clean.

QUICK POTATO GRATIN

Pre-cooking the potatoes and using boiling milk speeds up what is otherwise a slow-cooked dish. *Serves 6.*

900 g/2 lb potatoes
approx 450 ml/15 fl oz milk
salt and pepper, to taste
50 g/2 oz grated cheese
butter and butter-paper

Peel the potatoes and slice as you would for sauté potatoes. Bring to the boil in a pan of salted water and cook for 5 minutes. Bring the milk to the boil in another pan. Drain and slice the potatoes.

Butter a shallow gratin dish and lay in the potato slices, sprinkling with salt, pepper and cheese as you go. Pour in the hot milk; cover with butter-paper.

Bake in the oven at 190°C/375°F/mark 5 for 30–40 minutes, removing the butter-paper 10 minutes before the end of the cooking time so that the top is crisp and golden.

PARSNIP ROAST

Parsnips are a cheap and tasty winter vegetable. The cheese gives them a lovely rich flavour. *Serves 6.*

generous 450 g/1 lb parsnips
50 g/2 oz butter
50 g/2 oz grated Cheddar cheese
salt and pepper, to taste

Peel the parsnips. Cut them into short pieces and boil in salted water until tender. Drain. Mash with the butter, salt, pepper and half the grated cheese.

Transfer to a small ovenproof dish. Sprinkle with the rest of the grated cheese. Bake in the oven at 190°C/375°F/mark 5 for 25–30 minutes until nicely browned. It will keep warm without spoiling.

HONEY-GLAZED HAM

The traditional York or Virginia ham is dry-cured—rubbed with salt, saltpetre and brown sugar, hung up to dry, left to mature and, sometimes, lightly smoked over oak sawdust. The better the butcher, the better the ham. Your butcher will bone the joint for you if you find it easier to carve this way—in which case, make sure you put the bone in to cook with the ham. A whole ham on the bone weighs 5.5–9 kg/12–20 lb, off the bone 3.2–5.5 kg/7–12 lb.

1 whole salt-cured ham (uncooked, with the rind left on)
2 medium onions
trimmings from root vegetables, such as stalks and leaves of celery, leek tops, carrot and parsnip trimmings, outer skins of turnips
2.5 ml/½ tsp whole peppercorns
1–2 bayleaves
600 ml/1 pint dark beer
75–90 ml/5–6 tbsp thin, clear honey

Soak the ham overnight in cold water to get rid of excess salt—but only if the butcher confirms this is necessary. Wipe it to lose surface salt.

Wash and quarter the onions, leaving the skins on. Pick over and rinse the vegetable trimmings thoroughly. Lay a bed of the vegetable trimmings, peppercorns and bay leaves in the bottom of a large pot and put in the ham. Pour in the beer and enough cold water to submerge the meat completely.

Bring all to the boil, then turn down the heat, cover and simmer steadily, adding boiling water when necessary to keep the ham submerged. Cook the ham until really tender—about 4–5 hours, calculated at 45 minutes per kg/20 minutes per lb.

Leave to cool overnight in its broth (which can be kept for the pea soup if not too salty). Next day, drain the ham, pat dry and trim off the skin. Transfer it to a baking tray.

Score the fat into a diamond pattern and paint the joint with honey to glaze it. Bake the ham in the oven at 230°C/450°F/mark 8 for 15–20 minutes, basting occasionally, until the fat is brown and crisp.

Serve the ham cold.

Left: Quick Potato Gratin, Parsnip Roast and Honey-Glazed Ham —simple but robust winter fare.

CHAPTER 7

THE SPIRIT OF CHRISTMAS

The coming together of families and friends at Christmas happens everywhere in the Christian world, and the warm feeling of spiritual togetherness flourishes most strongly in the countryside.

Carol services and masses remind us of the true meaning of Christmas. Attending midnight mass and listening to or joining in the carols enhances the closeness of the family, whether regular churchgoers or occasional worshippers. Few can fail to be moved by a choir of angelic boys singing Silent Night, and hard men have been known to shed a tear at the sight of their offspring re-enacting the story of Mary and Joseph and the birth of baby Jesus in a children's Nativity play. These are the elements of Christmas that cannot be bought at the department store along with the lights for the tree.

Many of the customs and traditions which abound at Christmas have a religious and spiritual significance which is easily forgotten. It is worth searching out the true meaning of the traditions that we indulge in at Christmas. For example, these days when children open a window each day on an Advent calendar, many will assume that it is nothing more than a pleasant way of counting off the days until Christmas. Similarly, they may think that Twelfth Night (January 6th) is simply the end of the 'Twelve Days of Christmas' referred to in the well-known carol—or just the time when the decorations are put away.

In fact, Advent is a season preceding Christmas that marks the coming of Christ. It includes four Sundays—the first, Advent Sunday, being the Sunday nearest November 30th. This marks the beginning of the religious festivities in many countries and is also the beginning of the Christian Church Year. Advent Sunday is observed in different countries in various ways, such as the lighting of Advent candles.

In pagan times, Twelfth Night was a quite different celebration than it is now. A time of wassailing, it involved a lot of noisy revelling and drinking. It then became linked with the Christian festival of Epiphany, which commemorated the visit by the Magi, or Wise Men, to the infant Jesus, bringing their gifts of gold, frankincense and myrrh. In France, Twelfth Night is celebrated more fully than in other parts of the world, usually with a meal or party when a special cake called the *galette des rois*, or cake of the Kings, is cooked and eaten. Hidden in the cake is a single bean, and whoever is lucky enough to get the slice containing this token becomes the 'king' for the rest of the day.

Another European tradition is the Christingle church service, which has been held in Europe, particularly Scandinavia, for more than a century. Usually conducted during the days preceding Christmas, the ceremony is performed by children. Each is given an orange, on top of which is a candle symbolizing the light Christ brought to the world. The fruit is decorated with tiny sticks bearing sweets (candies), which represent the benefits of the Christian faith.

The popularity of church services such as this shows that there is a need for a deeper meaning to all the festivities. Without spiritual occasions of this nature Christmas could be just another public holiday. With them, everyone—whether regular churchgoer or not—can enjoy the true spirit of Christmas. Preserving this heart of Christmas is important in our modern world of commercialism.

Above: Choirboys singing well-loved Christmas carols.
Right: A magnificent stained glass window, part medieval, part Victorian, soars heavenwards in a kaleidoscope
of colour. The immense amount of detail in the stories told in pictorial form in a window of this size demands
plenty of time from the viewer to look, study and wonder.

A NATIVITY PLAY

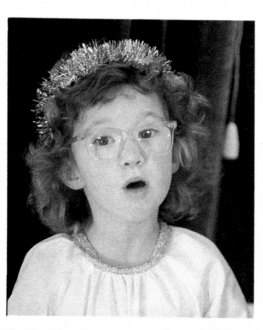

And the angel said unto them, Fear not: for, behold, I bring you good tidings of great joy, which shall be to all people.

LUKE 2:10

And they came with haste, and found both Mary and Joseph, and the babe lying in the manger.

LUKE 2:16

Every Christmas, thousands of tiny Marys are attended by shepherds in teatowels and angels with tinsel haloes, and at each children's Nativity play, with stifled giggles and stuttered words, the mystery of the Christmas story reveals itself again. Mothers stay up late sewing costumes and adults frantically try to coordinate the whole event, rehearsing reluctant or over-excited children and expecting a theatrical disaster.

But it never is a disaster. Instead, something almost mystical happens—a kind of solemnity tinged with joy which comes over everyone involved, from the tiniest woolly sheep or sheeted angel to the proudest grandparent in the audience. Every Nativity play is a triumph in its own way with meaning for all those involved. There is always that heart-stopping moment when a clear, pure singing voice rings out. A second or two of comedy is caused spontaneously by a shepherd and a king becoming

And she brought forth her first-born son, and wrapped him in swaddling clothes, and laid him in a manger; because there was no room for them in the inn.

LUKE 2:7

And, lo, the star, which they saw in the east, went before them, till it came and stood over where the young child was.

MATTHEW 2:9

entangled, or a tiny child lost and oblivious to the drama being played out around it. The Nativity play is still a perfect way for children to discover the Christmas story, while it delights and entrances audiences up and down the country.

The version of the Nativity play used these days is usually a simplified drama based on the Christmas story as it was told by Matthew and Luke in the New Testament. Adapted to suit small children's acting and memorizing abilities, it is usually short and to the point. The old Christmas plays performed centuries ago from house to house around country villages by the mummers, a group of local people heavily disguised and dressed in elaborate costumes, were far more boisterous and full of drama. Based on ancient myths, mystery plays, Bible stories and folk tales, the central incidents of the plays were connected with the celebration of the death of the old year.

THE SPIRIT OF CHRISTMAS

FAMILY GET-TOGETHERS

Every family gathering at Christmas has the same need for a cheerful social lubricant, particularly after lunch. Here is how Pearson Phillips, writing for Country Living, keeps the festivities merry.

Christmas is a curious occasion: we may find ourselves spending all day with people we know well but hardly see at all for the rest of the year. There could be a sprinkling of strangers, new boyfriends or girlfriends; not forgetting, of course, the ex-boyfriends and girlfriends. And there are those difficult old acquaintances or solitary souls who, from some ancient usage, always 'come to us for the day...'

Old griefs and pains lie, like dangerous rocks, just below the surface. What is needed is 'a temporary leave of absence from reality', as the sociologists put it.

Instead of board games that exclude people on grounds of age (too young to understand the rules or too old to sustain the concentration), why not follow our great-grandparents' example? Games were played with rules of such simplicity that everyone could join in, often with the most hilarious results. Such as a round of *Squeak, Piggy, Squeak* ... (Someone is blindfolded and led to sit on a cushion placed on someone else's lap. The sat-upon person squeaks and squeals like a pig while the sitter tries to guess who it is.)

My Aunt Came Home from India is good for dissolving dignities. Someone starts it off with that statement. Then the next person around the table asks, 'What did she bring you?' 'A fan,' replies the first, miming the action of fanning with the left hand. When this question and answer has gone round the whole table, and everyone is fanning, the first person adds an item: 'A fan and a pair of scissors.' The right hand is now used to make cutting motions. The third item could be a rocking horse, which gets everybody fanning, cutting and rocking at the same time. The more jerking and twitching the better. Last year, for example,

we had a fishing rod, a kite and a penny-farthing bicycle.

We usually do get round to charades in the end. The mimed book, film or play kind, as seen on television, is all right, but a full production is more fun than a one-man show. So I prefer the old-fashioned type, with dressing up from the old clothes box and lines of dialogue concealing the syllables of a word and, finally, the whole word.

For flagging adults in that nutty, port-laced period after the Christmas pudding and before the Christmas cake, *Smashums* or *Creepums* is ideal. We sit, facing our opponents, hands beneath the table, pretending to pass each other a silver coin. Then it's hands on the table, followed by the deadly choice of commands from the leader of the other side.

Smashums means slapping our palms down without revealing which one of us has the coin secreted inside.

Creepums, the fiendish alternative, involves making spider-like movements with the hands across the surface of the table, again keeping the coin hidden from view. (I'm told that there is a third command, *Milking Stools*, achieved by tucking the thumb into the palm and supporting the hand on the fingers, but that is a bit advanced for us.) The other team then has to decide whose hand hides the coin, if it hasn't dropped out already.

This may make us sound easily amused. But the passing game that really gets us going is even more basic. 'This is a spoon,' we say, offering an imaginary one to our neighbour. 'A what?' he says. 'A spoon,' we reply, handing it over. He carries on. 'This is a spoon.' 'A what?' 'A spoon.' Meanwhile we have started off another item in the opposite direction. 'This is a salt cellar.' 'A what?' 'A salt cellar.' It gets really good when there are five or six things in play. 'A what?' 'A rubber band...' The object? I don't know. We are too busy collapsing with laughter and observing each other in grave ritual to think about the purpose of the game.

Right: Music and games break down age barriers; grandchildren and grandparents join in the spirit of Christmas.

'TIS THE SEASON TO BE JOLLY

On the days before and after Christmas, to have an 'open day' when friends and neighbours drop by between certain hours makes entertaining a large number easy and unconventional. The best hosts keep the party going by providing copious amounts of warming punches and simple foods that need little preparation on the day. Dishes of dark, rich muscatel raisins mixed with almonds (a combination traditionally known as 'matrimony') are deliciously simple and memorable. Accept offers of help in handing these around, from guests who are perhaps unfamiliar to the rest of the group.

If the weather is of the crisp and clear variety, the energetic ones, particularly those down from the city, will probably enjoy a walk; lend them suitable garb and provide a scout!

The city streets are not conducive to gentle walks in the way that a group saunter down the lanes and across the fields can be in a rural landscape. The return to a roaring fire, chestnuts roasting (safest done in a metal roaster designed for the purpose) and a glass of mulled wine to take away the chill is the best way to warm up the voice before a traditional family chorus around the piano or guitar or even a recorder. It's a good idea to print off a few song sheets with some favourite carols and popular songs so that the words to the second and third verses are available. There is nothing more uplifting than group singing—it just needs one brave person to begin!

Above: Hot, spiced drinks like mulled wine have been associated with Christmas carol singing since the Middle Ages. (A recipe for a Christmas Mull appears on page 90.)
Right: The generation gap closes as family and friends make music and sing carols, with everyone adding to the feeling of Christmas cheer.

P I C T U R E   C R E D I T S

Photographs
2–3	Ian Howes
8	Caroline Arber
	(styling by Gabi Tubbs)
10–11	Jacqui Hurst
12–13	Jacqui Hurst
14–15	David Ward
16	David Ward
17	Linda Burgess
18–19	Jacqui Hurst
20–21	Tony Latham
22–23	Tony Latham
24–25	Linda Burgess
26–27	Pia Tryde
28–29	Linda Burgess
30–31	Pia Tryde
32–33	Pia Tryde
34–35	Pia Tryde
36–37	Pia Tryde
38–39	Pia Tryde
40–41	Caroline Arber
	(styling by Gabi Tubbs)
42–43	Caroline Arber
	(styling by Gabi Tubbs)
44–45	Sandra Lousada
46	Pia Tryde
47	Sandra Lousada
49	Pia Tryde
51	Pia Tryde
52–53	Pia Tryde
55	Pia Tryde
56–57	Pia Tryde
59	Julie Fisher
60–61	Julie Fisher
62–63	Julie Fisher
64–65	Pia Tryde
66–67	Pia Tryde
70–71	Julie Fisher
72–73	Pia Tryde
76–77	Caroline Arber
	(styling by Gabi Tubbs)
79	Andrew Whittuck
80–81	Andrew Whittuck
83	Linda Burgess
84–85	Graham Kirk
87	Graham Kirk
88–89	Vernon Morgan
90–91	Graham Kirk
92–93	Sandra Lousada
94–95	Roger Phillips
97	Roger Phillips
98–99	Roger Phillips
101	Roger Phillips
102–103	Roger Phillips
105	Roger Phillips
106–107	Kim Sayer
108	Kim Sayer
109	Tim Motion
110–111	Pia Tryde
113	Sandra Lousada
114–115	Sandra Lousada
119	Kim Sayer

Illustrations
Endpapers	Jane Newdick
5	John Spencer
68–69	Kate Simunek
75	Clare & Newman

Many people have contributed in one way or another to this book, and I am very grateful to the staff and contributors of Country Living magazine. Without their patience and goodwill it could not have been completed.

The following people deserve particular thanks:

CHAPTER 1
Peter Boardman, holly grower, and Miranda Innes
Judy Goodman, goose breeder, and Jocasta Innes
Alan and Elizabeth Smith, reindeer breeders, and Julie Davidson
Edward Stainforth, shepherd, and his family and Miranda Innes
and Sharon Amos for help in editing this chapter

CHAPTER 2
Lena Urmossy, florist and designer

CHAPTER 3
Lizzie, Amelia and Sam Staples

CHAPTER 4
Kevin McCloud, Sue Thompson, Chris Timms, and Lyn Le Grice. (For stencils and stencilling equipment, in Britain contact Lyn Le Grice, 53 Chapel Street, Penzance, Cornwall TR18 4AF, telephone 0736 64193; in the United States contact Stencilers' Emporium, P.O. Box 6039, Hudson, Ohio 44236, telephone 216-656 2827.)

CHAPTER 5
Philippa Davenport, contributing Cookery Editor to Country Living

CHAPTER 6
Elisabeth Luard, contributing Cookery Editor to Country Living, and Roger Phillips, photographer
Gill Smith-Moorhouse and her family and friends for allowing us to photograph their Christmas

CHAPTER 7
The Choir of Ashfold School, Oxfordshire
The children of Great Ballard Preparatory School, Sussex
The Way family and friends of Bigenor Farm, Sussex
Pearson Phillips, journalist, for his family Christmas party games

I would like to express my gratitude to Jane Newdick and Georgina Rhodes for helping me to compile COUNTRY CHRISTMAS, and Alison Wormleighton.

Francine Lawrence

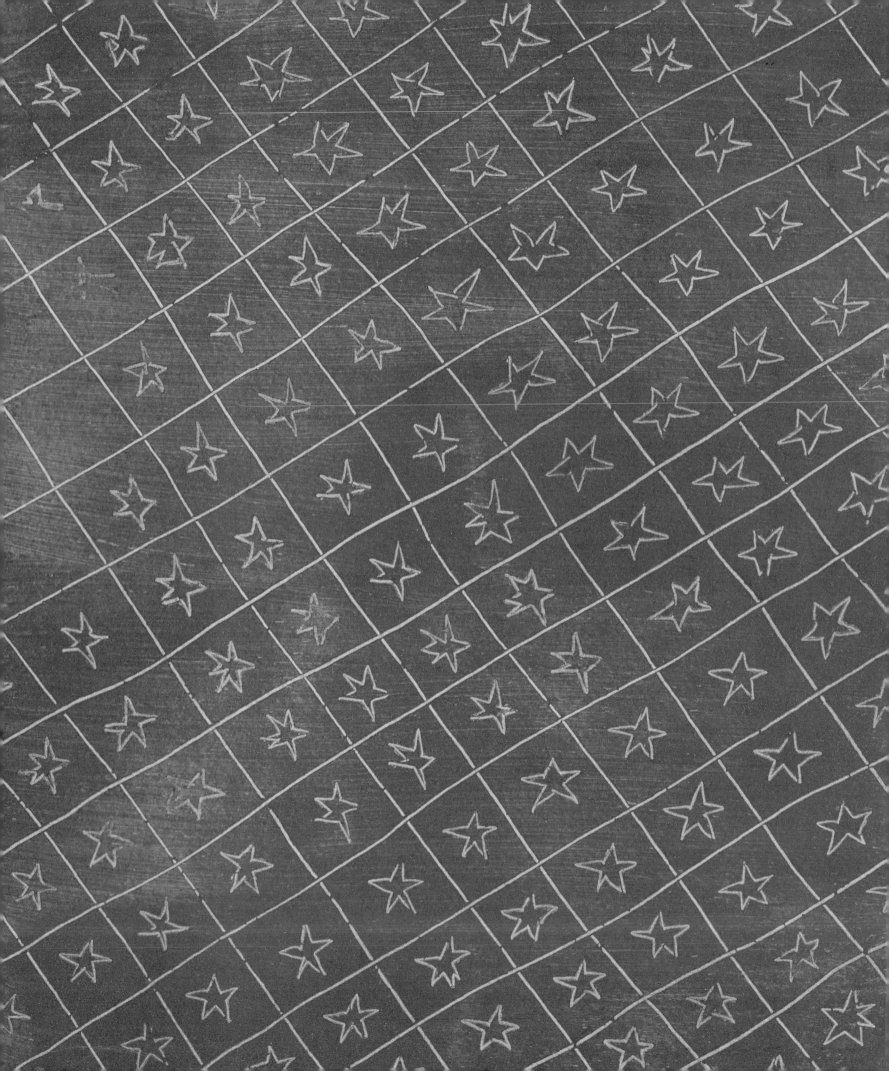